T R A N S M O N T A N U S

T H E   G R E E N   S H A D O W

Published by New Star Books
Series Editor: Terry Glavin

F6

THE
GREEN
SHADOW

Andrew Struthers

TRANSMONTANUS / **NEW STAR BOOKS** VANCOUVER

Come, let me tell thee of the Kingdom of Logres, and of how it was despoiled . . .

Legend of Arthur, 12th century

TEN years ago Tofino was a green tunnel, with Chestermans Beach at one end and the Maquinna Pub at the other. When I first saw the place I thought it was lovely — but I didn't want to live there. Too remote. Too rainy. No sushi.

In those days I was a typical university kid: Cadillac schemes, VW budget. I wanted to be a famous film maker, making films so great they would transform humanity. I had lots of ideas for famous films. But then I would skip over the difficult "making" part and get right to the good bit: me on Letterman, and the critics gushing:

"Raw Power!"

"FROM THE HEART!! ★★★★"

"Makes Spike Lee look like a spayed poodle!!!"

And so on. It was depressing. I could start off in the noblest directions, but I had no finishing power.

That summer I met a local crab fisherman called Leo. He was a big guy with long blonde hair and a Jesus beard, and he lived in a house he'd built on the inlet, close to town, with a giant TV, a Valhalla-sized stew pot and four freezers in the basement that he filled every fall with elk and moose meat.

I had just learned how to meditate, and I was trying to renounce meat. I liked Leo, but when he showed me his collection of moose racks and guns I reacted with typical buddhist/pacifist intellectual loafer disdain. I figured I'd better befriend Leo and rehabilitate him. Maybe even teach him how to meditate. Only it didn't quite work out that way . . .

Anyway, a month later, five of us were throwing dice in Leo's basement, hot-knifing hash off a blowtorch and firing handguns at a target on the back wall. The evening was progressing nicely when Leo decided it was time to trick me. He loved to trick his young pals. His favourite trick was to take you deckhanding on his crab boat, the *Clayoquot Isle*. When you weren't looking, he'd find a "safety crab" — one that had lost both its claws in some undersea brawl — and suddenly drop it down the front of your rainpants, sporting an evil grin. So far I hadn't been out on his boat, but in the meantime Leo decided it would be great sport if he exploded a paper bag right by my head just as I fired. That way I'd think I'd been shot. So he crept upstairs to the kitchen and puffed up an old lunchbag. Then he crouched at the top of the basement steps and waited.

My turn. I swung the gun up to eye level. Silence. Leo leaped . . .

But halfway down his head hit the drop wall over the stairs and crashed through the plaster. His body swung up under the drop wall until it was horizontal, then down he came, eight feet or more, and landed flat out, SMASH! on the cement floor, like a dufflebag full of beer bottles, his head jammed cruelly forward by the bottom step, sporting a terrified, rictal grin.

Utter silence. We were horrified. Surely Leo had killed himself. But to our amazement he struggled to his feet, staggered up to me and sort of crumpled the paper bag next to my head, feebly gasping, "Booo . . ."

Now, I was already as surprised as I was going to get. But what really stuck in my mind was Leo's finishing power. When this guy set out to do something, he got it done — even if he crushed his spine along the way. I figured if I could get some of that finishing power, my famous movies would practically make themselves.

I never made it to film school. Instead, I got married and had a baby. Back then, the green tunnel still meandered from the beach to the pub, and all I wanted was to live at the beach, drink at the pub, and watch my kid grow up exploring that green tunnel. But right around then I noticed the planet was spiraling into an ecological Armageddon taking me, my kid, Chestermans Beach and the Maquinna Pub with it. Clearcuts like sets for giant TRAC-II commercials were sweeping up the coast from the south. Every year, more tourists returned than salmon. I had to do something. So I decided to check out the local environmental chapter, the Friends of Clayoquot Sound.

Ghandi is Dandy
But Hitler is
Quicker

I'M leery of groups because of my family background. Yeah, that's right — it's all my family's fault. See, when I was a kid there was this thing in my head called the "family fuse". When our little clan got stressed past its breaking point — when, for example, we arrived on a new continent and our stuff didn't, or when we got chased in a dugout canoe by an angry hippo in Lake Nabo Gabo, or when something really horrible came on TV, like a BBC documentary about mercury poisoning in Japan, someone had to flip out. That someone was me.

It was a simple deal: my mind blew first, and the family would "reset" by calming me down and fixing me up. That way, we survived as a unit. I had the nightmares for everyone. And that's just the way I am. I cover the night shift. I take out the psychic garbage. Which was fine inside my family — we all had chores like that, and were good at them. But with a bunch of strangers? No way.

For this reason I approached the Friends with caution.

But it turned out they weren't really a group, any more than a bunch of Chinese peasants fleeing a tsunami are a group.

The leader by acclamation was a man called CJ. He translated *The Wizard of Oz* into Latin. He wore horn-rimmed glasses and a Gumby toque. He talked like the Village People. I was mesmerized.

Then there was Ron, a tall, handsome doctor from Australia, just fuming about life. During the cruise missile test he threw red paint on the police station and got a year's "good behaviour".

And Adrian, an impoverished single dad. At the same time that Ron was blowing his GQ top, Adrian quietly painted the local bank red and got ten bucks an hour. Some kind of yin/yang thing there.

And Julie, who was illustrating a kids' book in which the heroes were worms.

And Poole, a hippie who lived in a bus on Chestermans Beach.

And Dan, who grew up in Vietnam. Every day was Year Zero.

And Dave, who made long lines of candles on the beach to show you where the planets would rise.

And Kal, who lived way out in the wilds even though he had a real bad back.

And Richard, who had this crazy idea that he could make a living by taking tourists out in a Zodiac to see whales.

And Steve and Suzanne, who had raised a whole SWAT team of angelic ecotoddlers on a beautiful island.

And Jan, who could build an up-to-code house out of driftwood, glass, and silicone.

And Val, the High Priestess of Recycling.

And Susan, the deadly serious anthropology major. When they told her Bambi's mother was dead, she probably asked to see the body.

And Paul — man, he could talk. Clearcut/raw logs/Brazil/his Brazilian girlfriend/why she left him/depression/how to get permanent welfare — downshifting through the Alps of Chitchat like a Lamborghini.

The meetings were a little chaotic. We made anarchy look like a marching band. But the basic picture was this: Fletcher Challenge Canada (actually from Down Under) had just finished tearing trees out of a highway-side spot that later became known as the infamous Black Hole.

Now this known offender was headed up to the Megin watershed — an untouched wonderland, the place God would go fly fishing if He knew about it — to strike again. Fletcher Challenge was blasting a logging road along the rocky shores of Sulphur Pass. If they got through the pass, it would mean the destruction of one of the last virgin watersheds on Vancouver Island. Our plan was simple: head them off at the pass.

Blockading didn't appeal to me. I'm leery of war metaphors. And, anyway, the first thing I did out of high school was build a logging road up by Chetwynd. I vaguely recall stapling a metal tag to a tree with an eagle's aerie in it and wondering where the eagle would move to. What did I know about the environment? I got off the school bus and onto the crummy (which was an old school bus). If someone had shown up one morning and wept and hidden my tools and told me I was responsible for the hole in the ozone layer . . . well, let's just say it would have been the wrong way to try to reach me.

On the other hand, it seemed like an excellent idea to cause a fuss, get some TV cameras out to Sulphur Pass, and show the public what was afoot in the wilds. Remember, this was back in 1988, when most folks still thought the environment was the branch of government that dealt with highway medians.

As the day of the blockade approached, I agonized over whether to go or not. Finally I thought, "I will go. But I won't pick a side. I'll ignore the whole war metaphor. If I feel up to it, I'll just ask the police to arrest me, so I can throw my body on the pyre of civil disobedience without getting in some logger's face."

The big day came, and I was pretty alarmed. I felt like a volcano virgin. At that point in my life, though, I was cooking in a burrito joint for $6 an hour and looking after a three-month-old all night, and I was stressed. At least this was a trip into the wilds.

Early one morning in June a little flotilla of boats chugged up Miller Channel to Obstruction Island, which lies at the mouth of Sulphur Pass. There was a cabin on the shore, with a campfire out front and a biffy in back. As soon as we got set up, Steve threw a line in the water and pulled out a salmon. We cooked it for breakfast.

Then a second fish was caught. We hung it on a little shore pine for later. By mid-morning the shore pine had a dozen fish on it, and it looked like some strange allegorical religious painting from the twelfth century.

Three days passed. The tree of fish went from Breughel to Bosch, and began to smell. And a strange and sinister change took place in me.

The part of me that loved Chestermans Beach still felt right at home, but the part that liked to drink at the Maquinna, watch the strippers on the big semicircular stage, and fire off handguns in Leo's basement began to feel like a frog on a dissection plate. This caused big trouble at Head Office.

Head Office is what I call that Pentagon in the top room of my soul that guards my every move. Perhaps you have one, too. When I feel at peace with myself, Head Office is shut down, except for the occasional memo about scratching my balls in public. But when I'm stressed, depressed, or under attack, I can't even talk till my lips get the green light from Head Office. I had thought being out in the wilds would give me a taste of inner peace. In fact, the last time Head Office saw this much action was in Sunday school.

Fortunately, on the morning of the third day I'd had to put all of my personal concerns on a backburner because the cops and loggers showed up, and panic ensued.

I don't recall exactly how I went from Mr. Neutral to GI Joe, but by mid-morning I was on the cliff above the blast site with Kal and Richard, howling like a wolf between the toots of the warning horn while down on the road someone told the police not to let the loggers blast in case we got blown up.

It was a beautiful day. The sun shone. Insects buzzed. It was so quiet we could hear them arguing down on the road. Hours passed. "Hey," I thought, "it's working!"

Around noon Kal went back to the camp to get some water, and Richard and I began to argue about the Canadian government.

"They're a bad bunch of apples," he said.

Now if he'd said they were a great bunch of guys, I would have mentioned the smallpox-laden blankets they used to pass out to the Indians — or something like that. But since Richard was already running them down, I stuck up for them.

"Listen," I said, "I was just in TIBET." (Always a showstopper.) "In TIBET, they shoot protesters in the head and send the bill for the bullets to their families. Those are the bad apples. This government won't let someone blow up some rock a hundred feet away in case we get hurt, because here in Canada — "

KA-BOOOOOOOOM!

A ton of bedrock went up in smoke, along with my "True North, Strong and Free" speech. Richard and I hit the deck so fast we bounced off each other. Fly rock came rattling down around us. This was one hell of a war metaphor.

For the rest of the day we were chased through the bush and up and down cliffs by what appeared to be loggers with superhuman powers. Helicopters buzzed us. Cops yelled through bullhorns. It was an old-growth *Gong Show*. Then, suddenly, Vietnam Dan appeared from behind a tree and said the cops wanted to make a deal with us: we could just "come down" and they wouldn't arrest us. This did not seem likely. Dan went back down and told them he couldn't find us, and shortly afterwards five o'clock came and everyone went home. It was just like that old cartoon where the sheepdog and the wolf fight all day and then the whistle blows and they politely bid each other good-evening. By dusk, Sulphur Pass was silent again.

When we got back to our camp it was deserted, and there were court injunctions stapled to everything. We used them to light a fire. I huddled in my sleeping bag and let the night wrap its starry limbs around me. What a day. But at least the family fuse would reset itself by morning, and I could get the hell out of there.

The utter silence of the dawn was broken by the sound of a distant outboard. I paid it no heed until Richard went tearing past my feet screaming, "It's the cops! Run for it!"

I sat up. Right in front of me a Zodiac hit the beach. Five cops in bright-red survival suits spilled out. Still groggy from sleep, I ran into the bush wearing only my underpants.

I had imagined the scene of my arrest very differently. Back in town, I'd pictured it this way: me and Don, the local sergeant, would talk it over *mano a mano*. Then he'd nod and slap the cuffs on me in a matter-of-fact way. Since I'd arrived at the camp, a second fantasy had eclipsed the first. In it, I was dragged from under the bumper of a huge logging truck while cameras rolled and loggers cursed and my ecobuddies sang "One Tin Soldier" in the background. But this was like nothing I'd ever imagined. I was being chased through the bush in my underpants, and not a camera in sight.

As I marvelled at the difference between fantasy and reality, I noticed Pierre, a local cop, coming through the trees. He was tracking me, just like a Mountie in some old movie. Then I thought, "Hey — he really is a Mountie. And I'm his man!" I was trapped in the dark underbelly of the Canadian Dream.

In terror, I slid under a huge rock and tried to become one with the earth. It didn't work. Suddenly Pierre leaped on me from the top of the rock, yelling "Don't move!" After a brief cop/naked guy scrum, we stood up and said hello. Then we walked down to the protest camp, where he began to read me a court injunction the size of a telephone book.

Blackflies bit. The sun got hot. Tides of emotion surged through me: a desire to weep, a desire to laugh hysterically, concern that the charred remains of the court injunctions sticking out of the campfire made me look less than neutral — and Pierre was taking forever to plough through this legal mumbo jumbo in his Trois-Rivières brogue.

The blackflies got intense. In desperation, I began to help with some of the bigger words.

At last Don came over and asked me for my full name.

"Uh — John Doe?" I mumbled halfheartedly.

"No way!" exploded Pierre. "You're the one that done the funny menus at the pub! It's Andrew Sumptin!"

Always remember — be just. And if you can't be just, be arbitrary.
— William S. Burroughs

Andrew Sumptin appeared in Supreme Court in Vancouver a few weeks later. The charge: civil contempt of court. They were trying us by the bunch, and that morning about thirty of us filed into the courtroom.

The first thing that struck me was the size of the judge's desk. It was huge. It looked like the portable where we took Grade 10 drama, except with pens and notepads on the roof. I was quite intimidated. Also, a paranoid fantasy had sprung up around those burned injunctions. Already I could see a lawyer holding up the charred remains in a plastic bag. "Exhibit A!" The judge angrily brings down his gavel. BAM! "Thirty days!" My daughter never forgives me for deserting her. We grow distant. I lose her. I become a bitter, lonely old man —

So it came as a welcome surprise when the Fletcher Challenge lawyer stood up and said he wanted to drop the charges.

To my amazement, my lawyer stood up and said, "No way."

"My Lord," he began, "my clients do not appreciate being dragged here — lost wages — expense — blah blah blah bla-blah blah blah —"

Personally, I had lost all desire to do anything except escape. But I didn't say anything, and the trial lasted two days.

The second day was worse. It started with a little rally down at the Fletcher Challenge head office. We chanted "NO MORE CLEAR-

CUTS!" and handed out flyers that said "The Battle for Clayoquot Sound," and I'm not sure what else, because they showed up at the last moment and I was too strung out to read.

Just before lunch the prosecution rolled in a big TV and showed a tape of Ron, the fuming physician from Down Under. His year of good behaviour had ended that morning. By noon he was riding the drill rig at Sulphur Pass like it was a mechanical bull at a honky-tonk. There was a spontaneous burst of applause, which the prosecution cited as an example of our contempt. I guess it was. But the judge was mainly concerned with the fact that most of us were nowhere near the end of the road when we were arrested, except for CJ, who actually pitched his tent on the blast site. He decided to concentrate on CJ.

BAM! Down came the gavel. Fletcher Challenge had to cough up cash for my expenses, which my lawyer took in lieu of a fee. I didn't care. I was free!

There was an after-court soirée at Deadly Serious Susan's house in Kerrisdale. I got a six-pack and started pounding them back. I was so relieved to be free that it was like a drug. By the time the news came on, a mixture of beer, relief, and the prospect of seeing myself on TV as the White Knight of Clayoquot Sound had given me a cavalier attitude. When they showed the clip of Ron riding the drill rig, I wanted to be up there with him. "Go, Ron!" I slurred, waving my beer. Then they showed a scene from the rally at the Fletcher Challenge office that morning, and I appeared in the corner of the screen for a flash — but mysteriously changed. I was roaring my head off and waving a list of demands in some pedestrian's face. "Wow!" I thought. "The Nazi Brownshirt of Clayoquot Sound."

That did it. The family fuse went nuclear. Head Office shut down completely. Energies went coursing through my brain that I had no connection with. I dimly recall leaving the party with Jan and Poole, and Spanish Banks swirling past as I clung to the dash of Poole's Volkswagen, and much later I got picked up by UBC Security clinging naked to a totem pole somewhere near the Museum of Anthropology.

I Piss in Your
Gene Pool

WHEN I got back to Tofino, everybody else seemed empowered, but I was in a slough of despond. Not only that, but winter was approaching fast. The rain came. People took off travelling; some went back to school; CJ hopped on a jet for California; and I ran out of cash.

In winter, Tofino is a dead town — like Chernobyl, except with fewer jobs. The only thing going was the fish plant. It's hard to describe the fish plant. It would be so much easier if we could trade places. So let's do that. I'll read this book, and you get your rubber apron on. Welcome to hell.

7:58 a.m. Still dark. You splash through the puddles in the gravel parking lot and duck inside a huge metal shed where the rest of the crew is wriggling into their rubber aprons and gloves. They're a strange bunch. They live in the same small town as the Friends of Clayoquot, but they are very different.

First, there's Spock, a huge Native from Ahousat with very expressive eyebrows. The nicest guy in town — until his fuse blows, and then the cops can't get the cuffs shut on his old-growth wrists.

Then there's the Kid: seventeen, Axl Rose ball cap, beat-up Camaro, and a perpetually shocked expression, like he's just been slapped awake by bikers.

And the Desperate Single Mom: still pretty, but losing it under a barrage of babysitters' bills. She battles the lack of glamour down here by taking the time before each shift to bend her eyelashes at right angles to her head using a thing that looks like a cherry pitter.

And the three ladies from Port Alberni. Every morning they drive the hundred clicks over Sutton Pass to escape minimum wage. They read Clive Cussler, smoke millions of Pall Malls, and spend their coffee breaks winding tape around their worn-out fingers.

And Roland: a big, florid German. When he sees you, he winks. Then he nods. Then he grins, shrugs, scowls, makes like you're a truck running him over — Roland will keep these strange gestures up all day.

And the Boss. His granddad was an Olympic pole-vaulter. His dad was a varsity pole-vaulter. The Boss only vaulted till Grade 8, when three generations of crashing into the big mat accumulated in his brain and destroyed his attention span. Right now he's gazing up, apparently checking the fluorescent lights that flicker overhead. But really he's imagining pole-vaulting over the cutting table, then over the forklift, then over the three ladies from Port.

The clock hits eight. You and the Enemies of Clayoquot belly up to the cutting table. The door bangs open. Rain pours in. Out of the gloom crashes Spock on a forklift. He raises the forks and dumps 200 salmon onto the table.

Once, the salmon was a noble creature and its life was a perfect

circle. It was born in a clear mountain stream, swam through the blue belly of the ocean all the way to Kamchatka, then somehow found its way back to the very same stream where it was born. At the mouth of the stream it found a mate, and together the pair swam as far upstream as they could. Then she-salmon made a little place for them in the streambed while he-salmon guarded her back, and there they had perfect fish sex . . . because salmon always come at the same time. And then they died, right where it all began, and soon a thousand tiny fish swam through the cathedral of their bones. A perfect circle. Well, those days are gone.

The circle of life now begins when a guy in a green slicker mixes a whack of milt and a whack of roe in a five-gallon Chevron bucket. As soon as they can survive the salt water, the smolt are herded into a giant underwater pen way out in the sound. The pen is patrolled by a big hairy Deadhead with a gun. He shoots the sea lions ("Because they tear the pen walls") and the crows ("Because they eat the feed, eh?") and the seagulls ("Because they *bug* me, man —"). And between target practice he throws the fish tons of feed from a sack marked Not For Human Consumption.

Why not? Perhaps it's the pigment. You see, salmon meat is orange because wild salmon eat krill. But, incarcerated in their undersea ghettos, farm fish don't run into a lot of krill. So the feed is laced with orange pigment. There are two kinds of pigment on the market. The first is considered safe in America, but toxic in Japan. The second is considered safe in Japan, but toxic in America. Hmm. At any rate, they're both orange.

Or perhaps it's the tetracycline. You see, when a wild salmon gets stressed, it often gets a kidney disease that weeds it right out of the gene pool. Farm fish, packed into their submarinal death camps, experience levels of stress known only to welfare moms with migraines. You can bet their little kidneys take a beating. So they are doped to the gills with oxytetracycline, because, let's face it, without medical intervention, these little piggies aren't going to make it to market.

The fish know nothing of this. They swim and eat and shit until, one day, the feed that has rained down from above all their lives just stops. The fish farmer has cut off their permanent pogey to firm them up for "harvesting". They get so hungry they'll eat anything: pencil stubs, beer caps, folded-up tally sheets — you've found all these things in their wretched little bellies.

After two weeks of starvation, they are sucked up a tube and brought to the dock, where their gills are slashed and they thrash around in their own blood till they die.

This is where you enter the circle of life. As soon as they hit the table, you grab the nearest one and cut out its gills. Then you pass it to the Kid, who tears out its guts with a pop! and slides it to the Desperate Single Mom, who scrapes it clean and dumps it in the wash tank, where the three ladies from Port scrub it and weigh it and give it to Roland, who packs it in ice and ships it to Vancouver, where it is eaten by yuppies. But not by you. Nope. You would sooner eat an 80-year-old cancer patient.

Grab, slash! Grab, slash! The same gory three seconds over and over, like a time-lapse movie of hell. This is your workday. Once, you spent the day running through the tall grass in Africa, looking for something to eat and something to fuck. Well, those days are gone.

10 a.m.: Coffee. Five minutes to get your gloves off. Five minutes for coffee. Five minutes to get your gloves back on. As you head back to the line the Kid waves a joint at you, and . . . oh, what the heck. So you crowd into the furnace room with Spock and Roland and the SnapOn Tools Girl and puff away. Every day, the Kid says the same thing: "Is that all we're gonna smoke? I don't got a buzz yet." Because the only

buzz loud enough for the Kid to hear would be if you strapped his head to some great cathedral bell in Europe and let it swing with a BING! BONG! DADDY-O — Holy smoke. Are you ever *stoned!*

Back on the line, you realize you've made a terrible mistake when your third eye opens like a bad clam and scopes out the scene with awful clarity. Roland's face is completely out of control. He looks like Ozzy Osbourne biting the head off a bat. The Kid is ramming a broom handle into the jaws of the machine that grinds up the fish guts, trying to unblock it. It looks dangerous. The Desperate Single Mom is talking a Nantucket sleigh ride: ". . . and Nancy, my oldest, spent the week playing Super Mario, and I said, 'I'll break you of that little video habit, my dear — two hours of Nintendo, two hours of punishment, it's simple —' "

Your hands feel like frozen roadkills. Your head is one big skid mark. In desperation, you glance up at the clock. 10:18. Ten hours to go.

Okay, you get the picture? We can trade back now.

When I got home from work, my wife went waitressing and I got the baby. I was sorely tempted to hire a babysitter so I could hunker down in front of the TV with a block of hash the size of a truck battery, turn on, tune in, and drop off. But I didn't, because I had work to do.

See, when I was a kid, there were two paths that led from my little world to my mom and my dad. The path to mom was well-trodden. But the path to my dad led through my mom first. She was like a toll-gate on the way to the Land of Dad. I wanted my kid and me to have our own private pathway, so I got to work on it. When I got home, I would lie down in front of the TV with the baby and eat snacks with her and check out her little fingers, gurgle with her, and drift in and out of sleep. It was lovely.

But around January, she began to motor all over the apartment. She was a regular Danger Baby; if there was trouble anywhere, she'd find it. Suddenly, I couldn't drift in and out of sleep anymore, because every two minutes a bell went off in my head and I had to check that she wasn't hanging from a window ledge before it would shut off. I called it the Dad Alarm. It almost drove me nuts.

Then one day I was drowsing on the couch with a steaming cup of coffee. The Dad Alarm rang. Before I was even awake, I had grabbed the coffee cup and put it up out of harm's way. Then I groggily realized the baby had crawled right up to it and had been about to tip it on her head.

I was overcome with relief and wonder. Now, how did I do that? It was as if a whole new department had opened in Head Office, and it was in charge of looking out for the baby even when I was unconscious. How wonderful! Suddenly the Land of Dad seemed like a vast new continent, and I was filled with pilgrim spirit. I wanted to explore.

But there was a dark forest in that new land. Some nights the Dad Alarm went off every half hour, and I would have to get up and lay eyes on the kid before it would stop. Sometimes I couldn't get back to sleep at all. Then I would sit by the window and watch the rain pound on the docks. I could see the fish plant from my room. And I could smell the family fuse beginning to smoke. I could just see the headlines: "Dad Goes Berserk with Axe".

But the winter was passing. If I could just make it to spring, I could get on a fish boat and things would be okay.

My plans for saving the planet were on a back burner, but I still hung out with the Friends because they were my friends. One night at a party, everyone was talking about an eagle that had washed up near the fish farm. The Friends were suspicious. Maybe it was poisoned by the feed. Maybe even shot by a fish farmer. Maybe they would have to blockade — THE FISH PLANT!

Remember that Pentagon in my soul that guards my every move? All the alarms went off at once.

RED ALERT!
BATTLE STATIONS!
DIVE! DIVE! DIVE!

Of course, I knew in my heart of hearts that the Friends weren't the enemy. But a war metaphor is a war metaphor. I got an urgent bulletin from Head Office:

WAKE UP, BOZO! THEY MAY BE
FRIENDS OF CLAYOQUOT SOUND,
BUT THEY ARE ENEMIES OF THE
INDEPENDENT STATE OF ANDREW.
DIPLOMATIC TIES ARE HEREBY
SEVERED. THAT IS ALL.

True enough, I thought darkly. Categorizing these people as welfare hippies might be completely inappropriate, but categorizing them as angst-besotted middle-class urban refugees who are working out painful psychological traumas at the expense of the working man might be pretty close to the mark. If these people save the planet, I'm leaving!

CHAPTER THREE

The Hitcher King

AT last, spring came. The rain stopped. The geese flew overhead. The alders put forth their buds. There was only one place in all of Clayoquot Sound where the rays of the new sun could not penetrate: the fish plant. Unfortunately, that's where I was.

I felt very alone down there. I'd lost faith in the Friends. I'd lost faith in groups of any kind. I still wanted to save the planet. But what could I do? I was trapped in fish-plant hell.

There was one good thing about being trapped in hell: I cut to the chase. One day I thought: "Screw the planet — I'm going to save myself."

The first step was to find a better job. Remember my fantasy about becoming a famous film maker? Well, the fish plant sobered me up. It didn't look like I'd ever save the $20 million I needed for my magnum opus while working on the line. Plus, after cutting almost half a million fish, I had the attention span of a channel-surfing cokehead. A feature film seemed a wee bit out of my league. I decided to concentrate on something I could do in an hour with a budget of five bucks: draw twisted little cartoons.

See, for about a year I'd been having these visions of a city at night, full of odd little scenes, very dark stuff. I began to draw these scenes. They were so twisted that I was ashamed of them. But at this point I had nothing to lose. So I began to mail them off to magazines.

Clayoquot Sound is a fertile place. It's still the dawn of time out here. Things grow big, and fast. You could throw down a beer can and a Genuine Draft tree would grow by morning. So it was with my cartoons.

Right away they got published. Money began to trickle in. Spring blossomed into summer, and my cartoons blossomed into a regular feature. By June I was able to cover the bills just from drawing. By July I left the fish plant. Suddenly my cartoon was picked up by King Features Syndicate, the good people who bring you Nancy and Sluggo. I started getting cheques from the Hearst Corporation. Nice cheques. Big cheques. It was a dream come true. Soon, I thought, I'll be able to *buy* all the trees up at Sulphur Pass. Then I'll kick everyone out: loggers, environmentalists, media types — the lot.

But even as my artistic star rose, my marriage went into a Hindenburg decline. My wife and I started to argue about everything. The names of planets. Reaganomics. Badminton (which neither of us even played). There was a storm brewing all right, and the idea of breaking up terrified me. I'd never been alone. I'd moved out of my mum's house and in with my wife. Embarrassing, but true. And the idea of looking after my kid without a woman nearby — my god, who would grab the tyke and run to safety when the family fuse went off? And even if it didn't, I was afraid that I would poison the kid just with my maleness. What if, unbeknownst to science, the dark male heart shot off terrible rays that were poisonous to children, and that was the real reason men never stuck around?

It was at this point that I began to think about therapy.

I'd always wanted to go to therapy, but I was scared people would think I was crazy. Only now, people all over the continent were looking at my cartoons and thinking, "Wow! That Andrew guy sure is twisted! Mental! Cray-zee!" I figured I might as well check out the different kinds of therapy available.

Freud? Nope. His beard reminded me too much of my dad's.

Adler: "The will to power —" Hmm. You can tell he's German.

Jung: "There is a part of the human soul that remains in darkness, unknown to the conscious mind. This is the Shadow."

Bull's-eye! Of course, there were no Jungian analysts in Tofino. The nearest thing I could find was a woman called Cathy down in Victoria. She agreed to take me on but said: "Realistically, Andrew, how would you make it to the sessions?"

"I'll hitchhike."

"What? Every week?"

I said, "Listen, lady, if I can stand in a fish plant ten hours a day for twelve bucks an hour, I can sure as hell hitch 500 miles a week for my immortal soul!"

Before we set out on the therapeutic journey I had to learn a couple of things. The first was how projection works. The dictionary defines projection as "The unconscious attribution to another of one's own thoughts, actions or feelings." I had already noticed this in my life. Few things distress me as much as a person who talks all the time.

The second thing was what Jung meant by the Shadow. (Actually, I'm not sure if this is what Jung meant. But it is what I mean.) The mind works like a light. When I think about myself, my soul casts a shadow. The reason I didn't realize right away that it was me who was talking too much, instead of some other loudmouth, was that I'd put that part of my soul into my Shadow, because it was too upsetting to think about.

It took a while for me to grasp these concepts. But when I did, we set out on our trek into the dark forest of my psyche, where the shadows are deepest.

My life was full. I drew every day until three o'clock, then I took the kid until bedtime. On my day off, I got up at six and headed out onto the highway, fishing with my thumb in the stream of cars headed south to Victoria. Some days I got skunked and ended up on the bus. But I always made it by nightfall. Then I slept at a friend's house, headed over to Cathy's first thing in the morning, spilled my guts on her hardwood floor, and zipped back up to Tofino. I kept this up for a year and a half. I didn't mind the mileage. I knew from the start that what I was looking for lay a long, long way off.

As a hitchhiker, I cast a strange dark shadow. Here's what I mean. This is a story I heard about me through a friend.

It seems there was this woman from Tofino who was driving over the pass to Port Alberni one day when she saw me hitching. She never picked up hitchers in case they turned out to be crazy. But as she passed me, she thought, "Oh. It's that man who's always with his daughter. He must be safe." So she drove back to pick me up. But when she got a second look at me she got scared. "He's so strange looking," she thought. She decided not to risk it. But now she was afraid to pass me a third time in case I figured she was taunting me and became enraged. So she stopped at the Chevron and filled her passenger seat with boxes and pointed at them as she drove past as if to say, "Sorry, full up." I smiled and waved as if to say, "Yes, I see. Good luck on your journey." Suddenly she was overwhelmed with guilt. When she stopped to chuck the boxes she burst into tears. Then she dried her eyes, screwed up her courage, and drove back and picked me up. And I'm the crazy one? No, I was just hitching a lift.

Spring came. Summer passed. I drew, I hitched, I spilled my guts. Slowly it dawned on me that this fear I had, that one day a fuse would blow in my head and I'd kill everyone within a day's march was actually something that had been projected onto me since childhood. The projection had had an unfortunate effect on my blossoming psyche.

Now it was like there was a big guy with a knife standing at the entrance to my unconscious.

The whole setup reminded me of a temple near where I once lived in Japan. The gate was guarded by a huge statue of a demon. Of course, that demon guard didn't scare me much. But the demon that guarded my own unconscious scared me quite a lot. It took a while, but at last (sort of like that woman who picked me up in her car) I screwed up my courage, tip-toed up to the big guy with the knife and said Hi.

What was he guarding? Well, it's a strange story. Maybe you should make some tea . . .

I was born in Scotland in 1961, the only year this century that looks the same upside down. The astrologers say whatever's happening when you're born is reflected in your soul. Well, let's see . . . Jung died. The Berlin Wall went up. The world teetered on the brink of nuclear holocaust. But I don't remember any of that, because when I was four my folks moved to Uganda to teach. So the first thing I remember I lived high on a hill in Africa, in a house that looked out over hundreds of miles of the Dark Continent. When the sun came up it looked like the dawn of time. By noon the sun was so bright you could burn holes in the grass with a marble, then at night the moon lay on its back and sailed across the sky like a silver canoe.

Sixty miles north of the equator, slap in the middle of a nuclear family . . . It was hot.

My family were a wild bunch. First there was Mum, the warm, central sun: an adventurous attitude, cat's eye glasses, infectious laugh. She ran the show.

Then there was Big Brother, a sort of heroic character who was into pushing the danger envelope.

And Little Sister, who had a flair for the dramatic, like a Wagnerian soprano stuffed into the body of a four-year-old.

And the mysterious Dad, who played the cool distant moon to

Mum's sun. He was mainly around at night, when I was in bed. In my earliest memory of him he has no head; he's just two vast and trunkless legs of grey tweed with a booming laugh that issues from on high.

And Mickey. Part kid brother, part monkey. Seriously. His mom was roadkill, and we adopted him. His ambition was to sit down to dinner with us, with a knife and fork and plate; but invariably the sight of the butter would drive him mad with desire, he'd make a lunge for it, and get kicked out of the house.

And Buzby, the bushbaby. So small he could sit on the edge of a teacup and drink without tipping it.

And Wan Tom, the giant siamese cat who was born in the jungle and came to dinner the night we arrived. He was so lazy he'd lie in your lap and pee rather than get up.

And the chameleon, who one day ran up the sleeve of Dad's overcoat, changed colour, and was never seen again.

And the monitor lizard, who raided everyone's vegetable patches by night.

The tall grass was full of snakes. The jungle at the bottom of the garden was drunk with monkeys. Every six months someone would get eaten by a lion while staggering home from the pub.

Day and night were the same length. There was no summer and no winter. The chocolate milk shakes in Kampala; the red, red blood I found in my finger when I cut it open "just to see what was inside"; the cheerful old lady by the temple wall in Jinja whose hands and face were eaten away by leprosy . . . everything under the sky was braided together in a perfect circle.

When I was six, there was family trouble back in Scotland, and political trouble in Uganda. No one told me exactly what was going on, but Dad took Mum, Little Sister, Big Brother and me to the airport in Nairobi and put us on a plane, and we flew back to Scotland.

Once, Scotland was so thick with trees that the Romans gave the whole place a miss, and the rivers were so full of salmon that it was illegal to feed them to the hired help more than three times a week. But those days are gone. By the time my plane landed in Glasgow, Scotland appeared to be an ocean of sandstone tenements.

In this new land all the people were women. It was like an ocean of women. While we waited for Dad to show up we lived with my Grannie in one of the sandstone tenements. Every day Grannie's psychic twin sisters came over and drank a gallon of tea and ate biscuits off one of those three-tiered plates. I flew a tiny airplane through the forest of stockings and table legs while above my fey aunties gave a sort of emotional weather forecast for the week ahead.

I was quite happy in the Ocean of Women. The only thing that bothered me was what the locals had done with the circle of life. They had cut out the dark half of the circle and tried to throw it away. Of course, it hadn't really gone away — but it was banished to the fathomless depths, although it sometimes poked its head above the surface in the form of the Loch Ness Monster.

Now, it's a funny thing, but when the darkest part of a circle is cut out, the brightest part has to go too, to balance thngs. So the world became grey, and I moved through that part of my childhood like a U-boat sounding its way through a grey abyss.

At last my Dad got back and we moved to the country, which I thought would be chock full of wild animals; but there was nothing. Just an ominous stone monument a few miles down the road from my house that marked where the last wolf in Scotland was shot. It was depressing. Now the only animal in my life was a small bear called Orange Ted. Folks said Ted was stuffed, but he was alive. I was sure of it. I figured he slept by day and woke up at night. For a while I thought I could rouse him by holding food next to his nose so he would smell it and wake up to eat. I spent many long car journeys patiently holding potato chips up to his little black thread mouth. But it never happened.

Around the age of eight I'd had enough of the Ocean of Women. Folks who call our culture a patriarchy must have forgotten their childhoods. When I was eight and Mum was thirty, towering over me in a purple rage hollering, "I'LL HAVE YER GUTS FOR GARTERS!" it was difficult for me to see her as the powerless one. And it wasn't just my mum. Everyone everywhere was women. Teachers, shopkeepers, neighbours. The money had a queen on it. My favourite TV show was called *Watch With Mother*. The books were full of little girls: Goldilocks, Cinderella, Thumbelina, Rapunzel, Little Red Riding Hood, Dorothy . . . (there were some boys, too. But they were all called Jack). So when I realized the adult world was run by men, I was delighted. It didn't look like a sinister conspiracy of bachelors back then — it looked like safe harbour from the Ocean of Women I'd been cast adrift in at birth.

That's when I began to check out the mysterious Dad: flaming Yahweh beard, rolltop desk. He'd gone from having no head at all in my earliest memory to *being* a head. He taught all day at the head of the class. He believed in the power of the mind. He drove his body around like a forklift. When I turned ten he became the deputy headmaster, and the other kids called him The Head. I thought Dad was pretty cool. I wanted to be a Head too. But how was it done?

Around that time I noticed something new emerging in my own consciousness. It started like a little coral atoll and slowly rose above the Ocean of Women. The process was well underway before I realized it was my own personal Head Office. Cool. I could hardly wait to move in and set up shop.

There was only one problem. They had a rule in Head Office: No Stuffed Toys.

This caused a major crisis for me. I didn't want to leave Orange Ted behind. I mean, I'd long since realized he was never going to wake up, that he was in fact just a stuffed toy; but his little orange body was the last limb of the distant African sun, the brightest sliver of that perfect circle which had been inside me since the dawn of time.

I couldn't let Orange Ted go. My big brother tried to help by proving to me that Orange Ted was not alive, using him as an extra in the films he made. I remember watching with a mixture of horror and mirth as he set up the bed so it looked like a sacked fort in the Old West. Then he draped Orange Ted over the battlements, riddled with knitting needles, and panned the shot through the wrong end of Dad's binoculars, drawling the voice-over: "Yep. Looks like a real massacree down there . . ."

In a strange way, it worked. I began to see this little movie in my head: Ted and I were on two trains that were headed in different directions. We waved at each other from those balconies they had on the backs of trains in the Old West. Ted got smaller and smaller, until he was just a little orange dot, still waving, and the voice-over said: "They still loved each other, and they always would. It's just that they were headed in opposite directions."

Right when I moved into Head Office, there was trouble in Scotland. The pound sank without trace. There was a coal strike, and electricity was rationed.

Mum and Dad packed six tea chests full of blankets and plates and next thing I knew we were landing at the airport in Prince George, B.C.

B.C. was very different back in 1974. There were only two TV channels. BCTV could sum up the whole year by showing a bunch of old news clips while Mason Williams played "Classical Gas" in the background. There were so many trees around Prince George we had to drive through a five-hundred mile tunnel just to get Chinese food; so many salmon we could afford to mail tins of the stuff back to my Grannie.

In this new land all the people were men. Even the women wore pants and called each other guys.

Head Office was truly spectacular. It reached all the way into outer space. I was delighted. But when I began my family chores, taking out the psychic garbage, I found out there was *tons* of the stuff. It was everywhere: on late night TV, in the bars and pubs, and especially in the bookstores, usually in the back room. Piles of old *Playboy* and *True Detective* magazines, and a whole wall of Harlequin Romances, where all the men were called Clint. The best of this stuff was disturbing; the worst was utterly monstrous.

Eventually I got pretty scared, and decided to concentrate on Head Office. I figured if I could build Head Office high enough, I would rise above all the psychic garbage like the Silver Surfer from Marvel Comics. I put shots of Earth from space on my wall, I built space rockets, rode motorbikes and went skiing a lot. Soon I had developed a tough shell. By the time I was 19 I had a front line of defenses that made NORAD look like an old Gameboy. But inside, to my dismay, there still raged the Ocean of Women. See, my feelings, my dreams, my body itself, all were formed in that ocean. By the time I was 20 I was like some strange chocolate: crunchy patriarchal shell, with a soft chewy matriarchal centre.

All this made me very jumpy on the whole topic of sex. In fact, throughout my teenage years I never even dated a girl. I spent the whole time alone in my room, practicing. Teetering on the brink of manhood, I thrashed around clutching at straws. I even tried becoming a feminist. I tried to think like a female, in the hope that I'd end up getting to know one. This was a poor plan for a person who is up to his neck in the Ocean of Women. Things might have come to no good, but for the fact that when I was 23 I went to live in Japan for a year.

In Japan they had a third way of dealing with the circle of life. They cut it into two, like in the West — but they didn't throw the dark half away. They figured both halves were necessary. Best of all, there was a place for every part of the circle of life in their temples, even the most monstrous fragments. After seeing a hundred million people live that way quite happily for a year I began to wonder if I could build an inner sanctum like those temples, where the most monstrous slivers of my own soul could find safe refuge. The only problem: my Inner Sanctum lay somewhere in the depths below Head Office, and it looked a long way down.

But there was hope. You see, that which had appeared in Scotland as the Loch Ness Monster emerged from the depths of the Asian psyche as a serpent, coiled at the base of the spine. Now I could see a new direction: instead of rising into the stratosphere I'd dive into the depths. Instead of trying to think female I'd try to feel male. Carry the light of consciousness down into the abyss, and see what was there. And the best place to do this was right here on Vancouver Island, where the SuperNatural monster of the deep, although endangered, was still very much alive . . .

While I was uncovering all this stuff a whole year passed. Summer ripened into fall. Winter raged again. The Berlin Wall came down. The road over the pass got blocked with snow, the snow thawed, and the world came back to life. But even as the world greened up around me, my marriage began to wither.

My marriage was sacred to me. When I got married, I let my wife into the Inner Sanctum of my soul and stood there before her, naked. In the spirit of metaphysical *glasnost*, I told my wife everything. I held nothing back. I confided. I confessed. I ratted on myself. In the name of intimacy, I pulled my sins up by their stems and exposed their white taproots to her. Soon my Inner Sanctum began to reek. To clean out the stench, I got more naked, more exposed, I dredged up ever-darker horrors from the bilge until finally it seemed like I was making the stuff up just to top myself.

That summer, I knew things had to change. With Cathy's help I tore down that old, reeking Inner Sanctum and built a new one. There was only one rule in the new temple: no one but me was allowed to enter. Not even Cathy. Not even my beautiful wife. Inside, in the perfect solitude, I found what I had been looking for: the beauty of perfect solitude, and the stillness and mystery that beauty holds.

There was only one problem: in building the new temple that way, I had changed the essence of my marriage covenant. As soon as the new temple was completed, my marriage broke apart.

It was so sad. It would have been different if I'd married a rat-faced witch from Hades. But my wife was beautiful and intelligent. I still loved her. It's just that suddenly we were swimming in opposite directions.

That fall, my X-Wife and I agreed to each take the kid for half the week and got separate houses. At least, she got a separate house and I crashed on couches and floors and ended up in a bed-and-breakfast. My X-Wife did everything except the hokey-pokey to help me out, but life as a single dad sucked. I had trouble drawing. I went through a ton of cash, and suddenly I realized winter was almost upon me, and I had a two-year-old daughter and nowhere to live.

The rains came, and a woman who was leaving to winter in Costa Rica noticed my plight. She had planned to lock her house up; at the last moment she rented it to me.

I was overjoyed. I moved in with my mondo stereo and my drawing equipment and set up shop. It was a beautiful house, huge and old. Of course, it came with a huge old rent bill. I didn't care. I was safe for the winter and I had lots of cash and a quiet place to draw, and I had my kid half of every day. It wasn't so bad being a single dad.

To my horror, I found I'd lost the will to draw. And I'd been bleeding cash like a gored Vanderbilt. By the time I'd paid the second huge old rent bill and paid for the oil and the diapers and the pizza and the videos and the car insurance, I was almost broke.

A friend of Jung's once said: "The therapeutic journey comes to a natural conclusion when the patient runs out of cash." But Cathy was cool. She said we could continue on credit. Her meter was running, though. Things had to come to a head soon.

And that's when two shining angels of destruction showed up at my door. See, I'd put up a note at the local coffee hangout, the Common Loaf Bakery, asking for a roommate to help with the huge old rent. A few days later, this odd-looking hippie couple appeared: Neil and Leslie. Neil had read the Bible five times. Leslie was a Deadhead.

They'd come to Tofino to help the Friends save the rain forest but quickly alienated themselves when they showed up at the AGM bombed on tequila and naked. They moved in on December 5th with a bedroll and a huge box of bootlegged Dead tapes. Immediately, my life went into a tailspin.

Flat broke. In debt. Car broke down. Couldn't draw. Gulf War erupted . . .

Neil and Leslie were not afraid. "Looks like Armageddon," said Neil. "Yeah, man," said Leslie. "We better have a party. A Big Party! A WAR PARTY!!" (Insert theme from *Repo Man*.)

And party we did, while oil fires raged in Kuwait and Scuds sizzled across the desert and Patriots defended the Holy Land. I partied high. I partied low. I partied with my two-year-old. I knew it was not a good environment for a child. I knew that if the Welfare Lady found out about this, I was going to be an ex-single dad. I knew it could happen to me. Everywhere I looked, single dads were going down in flames. The details are always different, but one day the kid is just gone, and it's too late. Dad hits the bottle. He doesn't care. The path between him and his child chokes up with weeds. Soon they can only wave to each other. Meanwhile, the path to Mom becomes a superhighway.

I knew I had to pull out of this tailspin. But I was in my final descent. Just like Saddam, I didn't know how to stop.

Finally, my X-Wife warned me that the Welfare Lady would not like my free-wheeling lifestyle. By this time I was terrified of the Welfare Lady. I reacted badly. "Gee," I thought, "it's not enough that I take the kid half the time, I also have to pass an X-Wife inspection. Hah!" And I ratted on her to Cathy. I expected Cathy to be supportive and remind me that I was the Cadillac of single dads. But she said: "Single fathers have to be so careful these days, Andrew. I think the Welfare Lady would be very concerned."

I was devastated. The terrible thing about building up trust in a therapist is you can actually hear their advice, even when it sucks.

At once, the party fever broke and I saw where I was: hell. My home had become just like the fish plant, except with longer hours.

Amazingly, the very next morning the fish plant called and said they were desperate for fast cutters. Could I possibly come down tomorrow? I said yes.

I had been gone for two years, but down at the plant not much had changed, except the coffee creamer was now called "coffee whitener". A more accurate description of the product, I guess.

Once again, the fish plant sobered me up. Of course, the War Party was still raging around me, thanks to Neil and Leslie. It was strange and somewhat alienating to watch a whole roomful of people slowly get blotto while I stood in the middle like a killjoy Canute, trying to hold back the tide of revelry. Then one night, at the tail end of a major bash, with hippies and dogs crashed on my floor and rumours of gas bombs in Jerusalem, I fell asleep and had the strangest dream of my life . . .

I dreamed I was in a city at night. The city was in darkness. I was carrying boxes to my new apartment. I kept passing this thing like a big torch, the kind Tarzan would use to explore a lost temple. It was unlit, and stuck in the pavement in front of a pedestal. Someone told me if I could pull it out of the pavement and put it up on the pedestal the city would be lit up and I would be a hero. But if I failed, I would get 10,000 generations of bad karma. "No thanks," I thought, "I'll keep moving these boxes."

There was a gang of young men on the corner. Every now and then, one of them would stride up to the torch and try to pull it loose. But the torch was enchanted: if you tried to pull it free because you wanted to be a hero, it stuck fast. Unfortunately the young men could not leave the corner without giving it a shot. So the city was full of young men on street corners and older guys with 10,000 generations of bad karma. "No wonder it's so dark," I thought.

About the tenth time I passed the thing I saw a goofy young guy walk up to it. I grabbed him and said, "Don't do it, man!" Just as I was saying that, the Dad Alarm went off — and before I knew what was

MEETING THE ANIMA

happening, I grabbed the torch and put it up on the pedestal, out of harm's way . . .

WOOOSH! The city lit up like a birthday cake. A blast of sexual energy went up my spine like a rocket. Suddenly I was face-to-face with the most beautiful woman I'd ever seen. She had long golden hair and a slender, almost elfin body. And she was in love with me! We'd always been in love. We always would be. We were the eternal Archetypal Lovers. Everyone in the city was whooping it up and celebrating. It was our wedding party. I was overcome with joy. I embraced the woman. I gazed at her face, besotted, and she gazed back at mine, besotted. Miracle of miracles, this woman could enter the Inner Sanctum of my soul without destroying the solitude within. In fact, I could spend every day of my life with her and still be alone — because *she* was *me*.

When I awoke, I was in a state of utter bliss. I had somehow left my head and sunk down into my body. It felt wonderful. I thought, "At last, at last I've escaped from Head Office!"

I arose and wandered through the remains of the War Party, stepping over bottles and bodies, to the bathroom mirror. I took a good, long look at myself. And you know, I didn't have any dark rays shooting out of my heart. I was beautiful. No wonder my marriage had gone wrong, and my art, and my tragicomic attempts to save the rain forest. What I'd really been looking for in women, in art, and in the wholeness of nature was that lovely young creature in my dream. My female self. What Jung called the Anima. I'd looked everywhere for her except inside myself. And there she was, gazing at me from the mirror, besotted.

Of course, it didn't last. The world came crashing in and pretty soon I was reminded that I was not a lovely maiden with flowing golden hair but a Gaia-raping white male with a bald spot. My lovely Anima fled to the deepest part of the forest and hid herself in the shadows; but I knew we'd meet again, because I decided right then to follow her.

With that dream, the therapeutic journey came to an end. About time, too. I'd hitched 30,000 miles — right around the planet. I was about to turn 30 and I had nothing. I'd traded the lot — most X-Cellent wife, beach house full of appliances, artistic career — for a single morning with my Her, whoever She was. And let me tell you, it was the best deal I ever made.

CHAPTER FOUR

Escape from
Head Office

NEIL and Leslie, my roommates, were wrong. The world did not end. The Gulf War stopped, the geese flew overhead, and spring came.

After a war there's a general demobilization, when all the soldiers get turned out into the streets. In Tofino, winter is a war, and on May 1st, the hippies who have covered the mortgages on those big beach houses all winter get turned out into the bush. That spring, I was one of them.

As May approached, I knew I should have been out looking for a place to live. But since that dream where I'd met my Anima, I'd become obsessed with the idea of building a house for her — a dream house.

First I drew my dream house. It was a pyramid, like the pyramid on the back of the Yankee dollar. I had no idea why, but that was okay. It was a dream house, after all.

Once I'd drawn it I built a scale model of it. The model was very detailed, it even had cutaway sections of wall to show little batts of insulation. Then I made a hillside out of papier-mâché with real little shrubs on it, and sat the model at the top. Then I emptied out the living room and constructed a full-scale mock-up of each room and sat inside adjusting the imaginary furniture. Finally, Neil and Leslie said, "Andrew, would you just build the damn thing?"

So I looked around for a real hillside.

The first person to offer me *Lebensraum* was Ann, a beautiful motherly type who once danced the part of Yul Brynner's daughter in *The King and I*. She had already let my friend Jan build *his* dream house at the back of her garden. Unfortunately, she made a mistake about where the property line was, so Jan's dream house ended up on the neighbour's lot.

At first the neighbours were cool. Then they talked to a lawyer. Next time they saw Jan they told him to remove the "structure" within six months or they'd tear it down. Undaunted, Jan greased some poles and dragged his house along them to Ann's side of the line. The neighbours were so impressed they hired Jan to build *them* a dream house.

Ann wanted to help me, but her property was just too crowded. Anyway, I'd been burned before by getting involved with beautiful, motherly types with confused boundaries. So I switched to Plan B: Poole.

Poole, my hippie pal from the Sulphur Pass blockade, no longer lived in a bus on someone else's beach lot. He was now a land owner: he had recently stumbled into twenty acres of swamp, which he called the Land. His dream was to build a hippie commune there. With my history of group dynamics I didn't want to live in a commune, and certainly not one that was built in a swamp. But Poole took me to the very back of the Land and showed me a spot high on a hillside forested with huge cedars and hemlocks, with the blue Pacific sparkling in the distance. As soon as I saw the view from up there, I knew this was the hillside for me.

Poole said, "You don't have to be part of the commune, brother.

You can be alone up here — nobody else wants to build here because it's so far from the road and the hill is so steep. So you go ahead.

"And look," he pointed out a huge pine snag. "That will provide firewood for your first winter."

It was perfect. I wanted to be far away from the road. I wanted to live on a hillside. Out here, nestled in the green canopy, my Anima and I would be happy. So I agreed to pay Poole $50 a month and got ready to move to the Land.

The other inhabitants of the Land were a colourful lot. Like Jeff, a handsome Frenchman who came to Clayoquot Sound to cut shake blocks. For years he'd gunned his motorbike through the vast clearcuts above Kennedy Lake, chainsaw strapped behind him, like a heavy-metal version of the West Coast logger. But he'd seen enough destruction. Now he had built a geodesic dome in the woods so he could reconnect with Gaia.

And Barton, who lived in a round tent called a yurt. The yurt had everything: rain collectors, solar panels — even a 12-volt TV for watching *The Simpsons*. Barton came up from Olympia to help the Friends save the rainforest. Because he was American, he couldn't actually blockade. Or vote. Or work. But he had oodles of advice for those of us who could.

And Raven, who lived in the heart of the swamp in a hovel made from old orange tarps. He was always broke. He could never kick in for beer, because he'd just bought a boat and he needed the cash for a floater jacket. He didn't want to die at sea. The way he saw it, the beer would only cost you ten bucks; it might cost him his life.

There were also a few transients, who all seemed to go through the same thing when they moved to the Land. They'd build a tent platform in the swamp, get real inspired, and decide this was Eden and Poole was God. Then one night they would drink a whole bottle of Jim Beam and launch into the tedious details of how "Poole Pot" had betrayed them, he was a jerk, and they were "Outta here, man!"

I decided the real problem was that just like those young men in my dream, these guys were still stuck on a street corner in their heads. They couldn't make it in the woods, and they put the blame on Poole.

The whole setup reminded me of how I'd blamed my dad for all my teenage angst. Well, I was past that stage. I'd long since stopped blaming him and started blaming my mum. I figured I could make it in the bush. I sold my big stereo, bought some lumber and a propane stove, and dragged everything up the long muddy trail to my spot. I built a sturdy 16x16-foot platform, hung a big blue tarp over it, and moved in.

Living "off the grid" was hard at first. I felt vulnerable, like a soft-shelled crab. But slowly the forest became the real world and the grid became fantastical and strange.

One night after about a month I was lying in bed reading a cheesy SF anthology when a warm spring wind blew out my candle. I lay in the dark for a bit watching the trees sway in the darkness. I was warm and snug in bed in the middle of the forest. "Wow," I thought. "I live outside!"

I was weaned from the electrical and plumbing grid quite quickly but separating from the psychic grid took a lot longer. My first big break came when I went to my friend Brian's house to get a shower. He told me there had been a revolution in Russia. At first I didn't believe him. Surely I couldn't be that out of touch?

"It's true," said Brian. "Gorbachev's out. Army's in charge. Well, gotta go to town. Need anything?"

Hmmmm . . . Half the A-bombs on the planet seized by a handful of dyspeptic octogenarian cossacks? I was suddenly afraid. I ran to the TV — I guess I expected continuous coverage — but there was nothing on about Russia.

People's Court.
Click.
Sesame Street.
Click.
WHEEL . . . OF . . . FORTUNE!
Click.

Finally there was a commercial break and Yeltsin appeared standing on the steps of the Kremlin with ninety guns pointed at his head. "You can make a throne out of bayonets," he said, "but you can't sit on it for very long." What a statesman. Mixed in with the commercials, it sounded like he was hawking some cryptic sociopolitical laxative.

It all seemed unreal. So I went up the hill and made a cup of tea.

As spring blossomed into summer I was glad to have my forest sanctuary. They say small towns are emptying out, that everyone's moving to the city. Usually economics is blamed. But I figure it's actually fear of bumping in to your X-Wife and her new boyfriend when you go to the store to pick up some milk.

My plan had been to build all summer, but as soon as I was comfortable, things took a turn for the strange. I began to cry like it was a full-time job.

I held it in while I had the kid, but as soon as I dropped her at her mom's, I staggered up the trail and collapsed on the bed. There was a lot of grief in my heart over losing my wife, but beyond that I had to get over the idea that a woman would come and save me — my wife, my mother, my analyst. I was alone. I would have to save myself.

Months passed this way. I had no strength for working on my dream house. It was all I could do to scrape together some Mr. Noodles and find a candle for reading. Thanks to the oil fires in Kuwait, the heavens were full of crud. It was the rainiest summer in 70 years. That suited me fine. I lay amid the pots and pans in my squalid bush tent and wept while the rain pounded on the big blue tarp overhead.

By mid July I began to think I should call Cathy, my therapist. Then one afternoon I was putting in my regular sobbing shift when my tear ducts began to burn horribly. Suddenly a huge clot of mucus came down my nose. I sat up. I was still stuck to the bed by a string of weird, viscous snot. I had never seen anything like it. It was clear, hot, and hung from my face like half a pound of transparent mozzarella. "Oh, hell," I thought. "I've done it now. I've cried so much I've hurt myself." As I cleaned it up with a blanket a strange metaphysical Coke jingle went running through my head: "You've cried up the lining of your emotional stomach, you've cried up the lining of your emotional stomach." I had no idea what any of this meant, but as soon as I got that stuff out of my body the weeping tapered off.

At last I felt like working on the house. First, I needed cash for supplies. But I didn't want to draw, and the fish plant was closed because the wild salmon had arrived and everyone was out on boats catching them.

Now, it had always been a fantasy of mine to get on a fish boat, but I never had, because it sounded like a bad scene: seven days on a floating bad-karma emporium with a skipper who sports a hundred-yard stare and never changes his Stanfields; a first deckhand with a tiny head, long arms, and a threadbare Metallica T-shirt who croons "Inna-gadda-da-vi-da-bay-bee" as he gaffs each fish messily to death; and, between these bizarre ritual slayings, a vast emptiness of sea and sky, underscored by the uneasy silence of pre-Robert Bly men.

But the word was I could bag a thousand bucks in a week. So I swallowed my fear and put up a notice at the dock:

DECKHAND AVAILABLE. FAST CUTTER.
NEVER SEASICK. CALL ANDREW.

Next day, a man called Peter, skipper of the *Dawn*, came down the dock. He was an unusual man. Born in colonial India, he now lived in Ucluelet. He had avoided the "10,000 generations of bad karma" thing that is destroying the men of his generation by uniting with his anima in the traditional way: he married a lovely young woman, named his boat after her, turned over every cent he made to her, and watched with delight as she made a home for them, which he guarded like a tiger.

Peter worshipped the God of Abraham. He did everything like it was still Bible times. Remember in the Bible when King David had to choose a team of crack soldiers for a dangerous mission? He got the whole army to run around in the sun till they were dying of thirst. Then he sent them down to the river to drink. Most of them stuck their heads right into the water and sucked; a few scooped water up in their hands and drank that way. Now, you don't have to be Solomon to realize that a surprise enemy attack while your troops have their heads underwater can go very badly for you. King David chose the scoopers over the suckers. And Peter did the same thing.

He examined all the ragged DECKHAND AVAILABLE notices and thought, "This Andrew chap has very precise writing. He must have fine motor control. Just the thing for working the trolling gear. I'll hire him."

When I got his message I was delighted/terrified, and I went down to have tea with him on his boat. He told me I'd get ten percent of what we caught. He also told me that the sockeye season was very intense, like a seven-day war. I thought he was speaking metaphorically.

On August 8th we got the *Dawn* ready for trolling. That was also the day all the junk in the atmosphere from the Kuwait fiasco decided to come down at once. As I clambered up the mast of the boat, up blew a storm of biblical proportions. After two hours, it was still building. Water came off the ocean in sheets. Boats began to smash against the dock. Branches snapped off the trees along the shore, twisted up into the sky, and disappeared. Of course, I had visions of the tarp over my platform doing the same thing.

As soon as the boat was ready, I raced up my trail. When I reached the platform the tarp was still holding, but rain was running down the inside in sheets. The thin plastic was vibrating like a fat tenor's vocal cords, spraying water in every direction. I was horrified. My dream house looked like the inside of a car wash.

By evening, my shelter was trashed. This seemed like a bad time to head out to sea for a week, but I figured the storm was an early warning from Gaia: "If you want to spend the winter with me, kid, get your

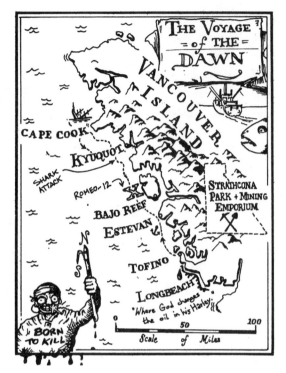

shit together." So that evening, when the storm abated from biblical to classical, I grabbed some sopping-wet clothes and headed for the dock. I slept on the *Dawn*. Next morning, we headed out to sea.

NEVER SEASICK? True, but NEVER BEEN OUT OF THE HARBOUR might have been more accurate. As soon as we hit the ocean swell I began to feel like I'd chased a bottle of tequila with a pint of salad oil. I was really up against the wall now. If they had to take me back, I'd never work in this town again.

I knew the old seasickness trick: keep your eyes on the horizon. Didn't work. Then a weird idea popped into my head: go down into the fo'c'sle and go to sleep. Let go — let go of my dreams of a thousand dollars, let go of my body, let go of my consciousness. It seemed like a crazy idea. But I was desperate. Nothing lay behind me except my dream house/car wash. Nothing before me but the rolling waves. I had nothing to lose. I crawled onto my bunk and shut my eyes. It was like being in the belly of the Twister at the PNE.

Amazingly, it worked. I fell into a deep sleep, and when I awoke, the nausea was gone. At once I pretended that I'd never been seasick.

We anchored off Hesquiat and ate lamb stew for supper. Later I curled up on my bunk while Peter and the first deckhand talked about their lives. The first deckhand was a young man called Ralph, fresh from a troubled-teen program in Vancouver. He had a goal: make a killing on the high seas, buy a Ford supercab, roar up to the rehab centre, and "Nyahh" the counsellors. Beyond that, he wasn't certain.

Peter talked about his childhood in India. Then about Hindu religion. Then about the cult of Thuggee, which worshipped Kali, the goddess of destruction. Thugs murdered for the spiritual high. Their favourite method was to strangle folks with a cord, which they called "a thread from Kali's skirt". As I drifted off to sleep staring up at the underside of Ralph's bunk, I wondered how Kali felt about this part of the world, where no one could worship Her — at least, not without getting arrested.

Day One

The time a man spends fishing is not deducted from his lifespan.
— Izaak Walton

Izaak Walton never had to fish for sockeye.

6 a.m.: I woke up, sat up and — WHAMMM! — smashed my head against the underside of Ralph's bunk, a ritual I would perform every morning of the trip. Then I drank some coffee while Peter showed me how to set the fishing gear.

Trolling is basic. You have six long steel cables, each with twenty hooks on them. You trail them behind the boat for a bit. Then you haul them in with a hydraulic winch. Then you take off the fish and throw the lines back in. Then you do that a hundred million times.

Day Two

6 a.m.: Whammm! I smashed my head in exactly the same spot, then I had breakfast, coffee, and put the gear down.

Peter did the driving, the cooking, and the dishes. He ran his boat like an airplane flight: every ten minutes he walked down the deck saying, "Can I get you some tea? A sandwich?"

Catered to in this way, Ralph and I were able to concentrate on the gear. The system worked very well. By the end of the second day we had caught 700 fish. My cut: $700! That night, I shopped in the mall in my head: a woodstove, windows, and tons of dried food soon would be mine.

Day Three

6 a.m.: Whammm! I staggered on deck, gulped my coffee, put the gear down and looked around. The ocean was alive with other vessels. With their stabbies down they looked like giant mosquitos.

The *Dawn* was part of a little group of boats that all had Christian skippers, called the Devil Dodgers (at least, that's what everyone else called them). The DD's had a code book, and when they talked on the radiophone they sounded like cops making a bust. After the big bite one of the Devil Dodgers, Henry, came on the radio and hollered that he'd got a Romeo Twelve at the Bajo Reef. Peter looked it up in the code book. 950 fish! This was shaping up to be a record breaker! By nightfall I'd made my thousand dollars and my list of necessities had swollen to include a motorbike, a 12-volt CD player and a trip to Mexico.

Day Four

6 a.m.: Whammm! Got some coffee and put the gear down. The whole sky went pink when the sun came up.

By 7:30 there were about 800 boats at the Bajo Reef. I guess they heard about Henry's Romeo Twelve. Worse still, the fish had stopped biting. A rumour went over the radiophone that sockeye had already shown up at the Fraser. Perhaps the run was over. Men who hadn't done well the first three days now faced a winter with no cash. Some would lose their boats. Some would lose their families. Their voices on the radiophone crackled with tension and despair. All along the coast near Bajo, the boats were lined up seven abreast and trolling west in files. It looked like an L.A. freeway.

Usually the fleet works together, but now it was every man for himself. Skippers cut each other off and got tangled in each other's gear. Around noon, one of the Devil Dodgers got into trouble. Some guy in a pogo boat began to squeeze him out. The skipper was a quiet, honest man called Arthur. He loved his neighbour — but he knew where to draw the line. As the pogo boat closed in, Arthur threw out his anchor. Now the pogo boat had a choice: veer off, or get in a big tangle with Arthur's gear. He veered off. A cheer went up from the Devil Dodgers. Then the skipper of the pogo boat got a gun out and started shooting at Arthur. Panic ensued. An RCMP bulletin went out on the pogo boat, and later we saw him running east with his gear pulled and his 10,000 generations of bad karma in tow.

At sunset, Peter stood on the deck and scanned the horizon. "This place is no good. Pull the gear, lads. We're going to Cape Cook."

I felt a pang of fear. Cape Cook is known for its bountiful fishing and its wild seas. But by this point, if Peter had told me we were sailing down to hell to fish for gargoyles, I would merely have asked how much we were getting per pound.

Day Five

This beautiful creature must die.
It's death for no reason,
and death for no reason is murder.
> — The Smiths

The Smiths never had to fish for sockeye.

All night, we took turns at the wheel. By first light I could see the great cliffs of Solander Island, with green waves crashing into them and gulls wheeling through the spray. We set the gear, and again we had good fortune — until noon, when the fish started to come up in pieces. There was a big blue shark feeding off the lines.

The shark was beautiful, indigo like the night sky. It lolled behind the boat biting at whatever looked tasty, like in one of those sushi joints where the food floats past on little boats.

Now I knew that as one of God's creatures, the shark had a right to eat, just like me. So for about an hour I practised Buddhist tolerance. Ralph, meanwhile, was practising with his gaff hook. Soon he had lured the shark right up to the transom with a pink salmon. He hung over the transom, gaff ready, his outstretched arm like a big stick of jerky. It looked dangerous. I got my gaff hook ready as backup. Suddenly the shark lunged, and before I knew what I was doing — Whammm! — I drove my gaff hook right through its skull. It tore free and swam away with the gaff sticking up like a wooden periscope. My heart pounded like a jungle drum. The great marble edifice in my heart that said HONOUR ALL CREATURES now had BORN TO KILL spray-painted over top. Kali had smiled upon me.

That night, the stars came out like diamonds. I sat on deck fantasizing about buying a motorbike. My hands felt like they'd been used to wedge open the doors at a Who concert. I didn't care. I was in fish heaven. $1,500! I felt a little uneasy about killing for money — but I'd eaten fish all my life. I decided the uneasiness stemmed not from a desire to stop the bloodshed, but from a desire to avoid it — to wash my hands clean of the dark part of life, never to touch the hem of Kali's skirt. But over the years, I'd eaten a lot of salmon. There had been blood on my hands all along — only now, I could see it.

Day Six

Sleep, that knits up the ravelled sleeve of care
— Shakespeare

Shakespeare never had to fish for sockeye.

6 a.m.: Whammm! Coffee. Gear down. By evening the hold was full. We ran down the coast to Tofino. At eight o'clock Peter said, "Take a turn at the wheel, Andrew. When it gets dark, be sure to turn down the brightness on the radar. That way the screen won't dazzle you, and you'll be able to see the lights of other vessels. Remember, these machines are fallible. Trust your eyes." Then he went to sleep.

When darkness fell I did what Peter had told me. Around midnight I saw lights ahead. Nothing on the radar. More lights appeared. Still nothing on the screen. I woke Peter.

He examined the radar and said, "You turned down the gain instead of the brightness." When he turned up the gain the screen looked like a firestorm over Baghdad. We were coasting at eight knots through a fleet of boats anchored off Estevan Point — kind of like driving a bus through a school yard blindfolded. "Now Peter will freak out," I thought.

There are good skippers and bad skippers. A bad skipper will show you what to do, hover over you till you screw up, then close in for the kill. Before you know it, your ego is on a hook, drying like a deer carcass in the sun. You hate yourself, you hate your skipper, and from then on you do as little for him as you can get away with.

Peter was a good skipper. He said, "That was nearly a calamity." Then he turned down the brightness on the radar and went back to sleep. I was amazed. And, of course, I became supervigilant. I hadn't watched a screen that closely since Scotland was in the World Cup in 1974. When at last I crawled into my bunk I was so exhausted I couldn't remember Batman's last name. Sleep came on like a street gang with baseball bats. My dreams were clogged with ice and salmon.

But I was happy.

Day Seven

On the seventh day, God rested.
— Genesis

God never had to fish for sockeye. On the seventh day, the *Dawn* listed into Tough City, heavy with salmon. I showered on the dock, which was rolling under my feet. By the time I had the fish scales out of my hair, Peter had a cheque ready. $1,835!

Yowza! Next day, the cash registers in town rang like wedding bells. I bought a stove, glass, tar paper — everything I needed for building, and all through August and September I worked on my dream house.

The mudpie summer mellowed into a warm, dry autumn. The evenings were long, and full of amber light. As my walls climbed towards the peak of the pyramid I wondered if this was how a crab felt as its new shell hardened.

Early in October I hooked up my woodstove and went to visit Poole at the front of the Land. I asked him to help me fell the big pine snag he'd promised me for firewood. Poole said: "Firewood? Oh, no no no. I'm going to mill that tree into boards for my house. I don't want the forest around your place to turn into a woodlot. I want you to carry every stick of firewood up that hill!"

Betrayed! Of course, I knew in my heart Poole wasn't a bad human being. Just a bad skipper. I decided instead of making him into the bad guy, I would be bad. So I went and found Jeff and told him my problems. Jeff nodded knowingly and pulled his chainsaw from under his dome. It had a 36-inch bar. "Wow," I thought, "this guy's been worshipping Kali on the sly."

We walked right up my trail and felled the huge pine. The thundering crash reverberated through the Land. "What a great sound," I thought: "the sound of firewood!"

We went back to Jeff's place to have a beer, and on the way we ran into Poole. He'd heard the crash. He was kind of upset. And by the way, when was I going to pay rent? It had been six months since I moved to the Land.

"Soon, soon," I said. What a fibber (it's now been four years and I still haven't paid). I guess I could come up with a list of reasons for not kicking in. #1: By building a house, I was improving the value of the Land. #2: Poole wanted to buck the system. In my case, Poole *was* the system. #3: It's all Native land — and so on. But the real reason was simple: I didn't feel like it. What I felt like was getting all that firewood put away for the winter.

And as I was splitting the pine wood and stacking it under the house, the rains came.

The Dark Star

BY the end of October, my dream house looked great. I had a bedroom upstairs, a nuptial chamber for me and my Anima with a huge bed made from cedar three-by-twelves. My kid had a little nook off the living room with her dolls and stuffed toys (including Orange Ted, who had been in a box at my folks' house) lined up on the bed and a Rupert poster on the wall. I made her a swing in the living room, we got a kitten, and when the storms howled outside, we drank cocoa by the wood stove and read Beatrix Potter books.

The roof over my bed was still plastic. I needed cash to fix it before the winter storms hit but I'd spent all my sockeye money. So I went down to the dock to look for work.

It was pretty quiet down there. The salmon fleet was tied up for the winter and the skippers had flown to the Philippines to get cheap dental work. I didn't want to go back to the fish plant, so I was delighted when the wharfinger told me a guy called Bob was looking for a deckhand to go shrimping with him on his boat, the *Dark Star*.

I liked the look of Bob: ruddy complexion that spoke of years on the water; shades by Vuarnet; hair by Medusa. He was over six feet tall and was missing the ring finger on his left hand. His boat had a metal hull that was painted green. It boomed when I climbed down into the engine room. Bob tinkered with the engine for a bit then said: "I tell ya, Andrew, it's been a tense season. The net wasn't fishing right all summer. But I think I've got it figured out. There's time for one more trip before the winter storms set in. Are you interested?"

I said yes. So we filled the hold of the *Dark Star* with ice and ran 30 miles out to Clayoquot Canyon, an undersea rift 8,000 feet deep. Of course, there are no shrimp down there — Bob just liked to drive over the edge so the sounder went BEEP! BEEP! BEEEOOOOOO-OOooooop! The shrimp live on the mudflats above the canyon. It was late evening by the time we got out there. Bob shut down the engine and we ate supper surrounded by inky darkness. Only the voice of the weatherman on the radio reminded us that we were not the last men on Earth.

After supper, we had a few beers and chatted. Bob was a typical west coaster. He'd logged and fished since he left school. All he wanted was to be his own man.

We had another beer and pretty soon we were talking about death. Then about ghosts. Then about those circles in wheat fields. Then about pyramids. Bob was Mr. Rational. He figured ghosts were a kind of mirage. Those crop circles were made by two old farmers with a log. Pyramids were smaller at the top because the Egyptians ran out of slaves. And so on. He figured it was a kind of mental illness to believe in something when you had no proof. A few more beers and we were talking about mental illness. Then about how Bob was mentally ill, and had been for years.

"But now I found this great medication, and it's changed my life! Here — I'll show you!" He leaped up and began rummaging through a drawer. I decided to go and lie down.

I squeezed past Bob and climbed down into the fo'c'sle. I lay on my bunk, listening to the dark waves slap against the hull, inches away.

Suddenly Bob thrust his head into the fo'c'sle and shook a scruffy little Pharmasave bottle at me. "See!" he said. "I am not ashamed to say to you, Andrew, that I am mentally ill!"

Because the fo'c'sle was lower than the cabin, he was hanging almost upside down as he said this. Blood rushed to his head, making the veins across his temples bulge horribly. I suppressed an insane desire to reach up and pop them like kelp balls. I stretched and yawned showily. "Gee, Bob," I said, "we should get some sleep, eh?"

Bob grinned. "You go ahead," he said. "I have insomnia. I never sleep."

Next morning, Bob showed me how to set the shrimp net. It was like a giant green stocking with a pole across the mouth to keep it open. There was a drum at the back of the *Dark Star* with a long rope wound round it; Bob tied the end of the rope to the pole at the front of the net and started the motor on the drum. It rolled, played out rope, and down went the whole shebang. Then we went inside and played chess.

Two hours later, we went back on deck. Bob reversed the motor on the drum and up came the net with half a ton of shrimp in it. I was impressed. This was a gentleman's fishery — it was like getting paid to play chess!

To get the shrimp on board, Bob tied a rope to the net and ran it up through an overhead pulley, then down to a motorized spool on the deck. He called it the "niggerhead". Then he apologized. "Sorry. I guess that's racist. The proper name is capstan." I was impressed by his political correctness, but a little while later he called the pink bag of air he used for a dock bumper a "Scotchman" and no apology was forthcoming.

Anyway, Bob wound the rope around the capstan and turned on the hydraulics. The net rose slowly alongside the boat, with water gushing in all directions. Suddenly there was a loud PING! and the wheel shot out of the overhead pulley and bit a chunk out of the gunwale where it hit. "We better fix that," said Bob. But we didn't. We played more chess.

Bob was a hot chess player. But when the pressure was on, his mind went to pieces and the pieces fought with each other. His boat was like that, too. It was functional, but there was a lot of duct tape holding the pieces together.

When we were hauling the net up from the ocean floor the second time, the motor on the drum suddenly blew apart. The drum came off its axle and jammed tight. Now Bob's $5,000 net was stuck 200 feet under the boat.

Bob decided to lower the net to the bottom on a long rope with a float tied to the end and go get the drum fixed. The only piece of rope long enough was the one on the drum, so Bob began unwinding it by hand. Soon the rope was one big snarl. Bob began to panic. He tugged and pulled at the sodden, freezing mass of knots, grunting and whimpering "Oh no, oh no, oh no," in a high, quavery voice while his face went from ruddy to crimson to purple and yellow circles appeared under his eyes. He looked like Yosemite Sam having a stroke. Maybe he saw the hopeless tangle as a metaphor for his life. I sure did.

At last he got it unsnarled. Then he gathered together all the Scotchmen he had on board and looped one end of the rope through all of them. He tied the other end to the rope still attached to the net, threw the Scotchmen overboard, cut the line where it was still attached to the drum, and watched as everything went down. If he hadn't used enough rope, the net would pull the Scotchmen under and we'd be screwed. But the little clan of Scotchmen continued to bob happily on the waves. Bob breathed a huge sigh of relief and we ran in to Tough City.

As soon as we hit the dock, Bob jumped in his truck and tore off to Steveston for drum parts. I lay on my bunk and listened to the election returns. It was October 19th, 1991 — the day the Socreds got nuked. Mike "Don't Log the Carmanah" Harcourt was our new skipper. "Wow," I thought. "The Friends will be so happy."

Next day, Bob showed up and fixed the drum and said, "Let's get the net!"

"Don't you want to sleep?" I asked. His eyes looked like raw eggs floating in ketchup.

"To be honest, Andrew," he said, "I haven't slept in years." And out we went again.

Amazingly, the Scotchmen were still where we'd left them. When we hauled the net up, it was full of rotting shrimp. It reeked like the whole Socred caucus had crawled in there to die. We emptied it, reset it, and went to play chess.

As I got to know Bob I found I liked him a lot. Under all that cholesterol there was a really good skipper. He knew everything there was to know about shrimp. When he described how his net worked it was like he was down on the ocean floor with it, watching the shrimp rise from the mud flats. But giant slabs of hypertension kept falling on him out of the sky. Family feuds. Falling prices. Fewer shrimp. He didn't need David Suzuki to tell him that something had gone horribly wrong with the marriage between humans and nature.

For three days everything went smoothly. But every time we winched the net aboard, the overhead pulley creaked ominously. Now that the wheel was gone, the rope was running over the cotter pin. Every time, Bob glanced up and said, "We should get on that." But we didn't. We played more chess.

Two days later the sun rose into a perfectly blue sky. The radio said there was a storm coming, a big one. Bob looked at the sky and decided to set the net one last time.

On deck, I could see the vast wilderness of Vancouver Island marching from north to south in an unbroken wall of mountains, forests, and inlets. Hundreds of birds hovered over the *Dark Star*: albatross, shearwaters, and strange offshore gulls I'd never seen before. Then a dolphin breached off the port bow, then three at once, then thirty. They flashed like shooting stars through the waves around the boat. I drank it all in. It seemed like our bad luck was over.

While the net loaded up with shrimp, we ate breakfast and drank coffee. But when we hauled the net up we made a terrible discovery. There was a dead dolphin in amongst the shrimp. It must have swum in while we were setting the net, been dragged down to 80 fathoms, and expired while we ate our porridge. I was horrified. Having shark blood on my hands was one thing, but dolphins are my favourite animal. When I was a kid, I wanted to be the scientist who decoded their language of clicks, then become a sort of interspecies ambassador and spend my life frolicking with them under the waves . . . just me and the dolphins (and Jacqueline Bisset in a white T-shirt).

"Well," I thought as I dragged the lifeless carcass on deck, "I've finally made contact with the dolphins." My hands felt like guns.

Bob was equally dismayed. He went to make some tea. I sat with the body for a bit. After a while, I thought, "Well, I killed it. I guess I should eat it. Have a dolphin feast at Leo's house." The idea of my pals chowing down happily on the exotic flesh cheered me up a bit. They'd think, "Wow — Andrew's quite the fisherman, yes, sir! He bagged himself a dolphin!" Barbaric, I know, but what was I to do? Have it cremated? So I tied a line round its tail and hung it off the port gunwale. Then we winched the killer net on board.

When Bob turned on the hydraulics, the capstan grunted and the net began to rise. Then it stopped and just hung there. Then a terrible tearing sound cut through the salt air. Bob and I glanced around in terror. Something had gone haywire.

Then, to our amazement, the capstan tore itself loose from the deck and rose into the air, with the black hydraulic hoses uncoiling beneath it like spindly legs as it rose. It reared up, its skinny black legs twitching horribly, its head turning round and round. I couldn't figure out what was going on. It looked like it was coming to life. There was a loud crack. The capstan's head snapped back and green hydraulic fluid spewed in an arc from its mouth. And Bob, Mr. Rational, stared at the thing with an expression of pure, childlike terror distorting his purple features. He threw himself back against the transom, hands over his face, and howled something like: "OH, MY GOD! IT'S IN THE HYDRAULICS!"

Up till that moment, Head Office was still in control. I knew, even though the capstan appeared to be possessed by Satan, that it was just a piece of machinery gone berserk. But when my skipper screamed, a chill ran through me and the flickering light of reason in my soul was snuffed out like a candle. The boys in Head Office were left cowering in the dark. But the irrational animal I keep locked away at the base of my spine knew exactly what was going down: the niggerhead was coming to get me.

I howled. I tap-danced backwards across the slippery deck like I was ramming Fred Flintstone's car into reverse, and smashed into the cabin door. The niggerhead bucked and writhed in a wild jungle dance spraying green venom everywhere, then — SNAP! — the shrimp net fell on it from above, flattening it against the deck, and the terrible tearing noise stopped.

Once everything had calmed down, we were able to figure out what had happened. The rope had finally snagged on the cotter pin and jammed in the overhead pulley. The capstan kept tightening the rope until it tore itself loose from the deck, then began to wind itself up the rope toward the pulley, giving it a puppet-like appearance. The hydraulic hoses unwound till they were stretched tight, then split, gushing hydraulic fluid. Finally, the rope snapped and everything came down at once.

Now that the danger was over, we saw the humour in the situation. We began to laugh. As we put away the gear and prepared to run in to port, we each retold the story from our own point of view and laughed even harder. Soon we were in hysterics. Bob stood at the wheel with his big magnetic coffee cup on the dash and howled till he cried; I lay on my bunk and laughed till I was in pain.

Outside, the storm descended on us. We took a big green wave over the bow. It threw me right out of my bunk. I just laughed harder. The third time this happened, I wondered briefly where the survival suits were — probably down in the engine room under a huge pile of Snap-On tools. I went upstairs and took a turn at the wheel, and every time Bob and I made eye contact, there was another fit of hysterics.

We got our buns kicked all the way in to port. Twenty miles. At last we reached the dock, and safety. But when I looked for the dolphin's body, the waves had washed it overboard. It was gone.

I said good-bye to Bob, got my kid, and headed up the trail to my dream house. I'd been gone a week. The place was damp and chilly. But I got the wood stove blazing and we ate supper while the storm raged. Winter had arrived.

When God
Was Your Mom

WHEN winter got serious my big carnivorous pal Leo made it clear I was welcome to crash on his couch any time the woods got too rough. Leo was on a bit of a downer right then: he had lost his boat and was logging again, this time on the other side of the island. He wasn't around much. But he had rented out all the bedrooms in his house to young guys, so there was a perpetual party going on, and the stew pot was always full. I was very grateful to him for his kindness — but what I really wanted was to sleep in my own bed, and get a stewpot of my own.

Soon my shrimping cash was spent. Reluctantly I signed up at the fish plant, where not much had changed, except the coffee whitener was now called "coffee top." And it's true — it does go on top. Also, the management had decided we would look more professional if we wore white lab coats, like scientists. It was a typical head office decision. For a week we looked snazzy. Then the lapels curled and the cuffs went green from fish bile, and by Christmas we looked like the sort of scientists who build doomsday devices in their basements.

I have never been as broke as I was that winter. At first I didn't mind being broke, because I had the kid to play with. We got into the simple pleasures of life. And when I say simple, I mean free. On sunny days I sat at the little playground across from city hall for hours watching my kid go back and forth on the swings, wondering if the stone bench was giving me hemorrhoids. On rainy days we did arts and crafts. (I soon found out why there was a sign at the daycare that said "PLEASE Take Home Your Child's Artwork!" Four-year-olds shoot the stuff out of their wrists like Spiderman shoots webs. There must be whole landfills of the stuff. I always thought I'd treat each egg carton sculpture like it belonged in the Louvre; yet I found myself guiltily burning my kid's great art in the woodstove at night, just to clear some floorspace.) In the evenings we visited friends with VCRs, or went to the library and basked in the free fluorescent lights.

It really was fun. And when I'd fed the little tyke and she was crashed in her nook, I'd take a peek at her small, peaceful face, and my belly would glow like a thousand woodstoves.

Of course, it wasn't like the Brady Bunch. Pretty soon I understood why my mum had yelled at me so much. It seems to be a kid's job to push your limits, like an emotional test pilot. Around Christmas I realized I no longer had the heart to blame my mum for all my angst. It was scary. I was running out of scapegoats fast. What was I going to blame for my pain? The weather?

They say that was the rainiest December since records began. Of course, they're always saying that. Tofino has the highest growth rate and birth rate "per capita" in Canada — and so does every other small town I ever lived in. But this time I believed it. Just after winter solstice there were seven storms, back to back. I hunkered down by the woodstove and watched them box the compass. I had built against the southeast wind, where all the rain comes from, so that wall was fine. But when it stormed from the northwest the whole house shook, and the trees out front swished around like kelp in the surf. The roof leaked right on the bed, my chainsaw went on the fritz and my trail became a creek. To get home I had to put my kid on my shoulders and wade up it while she jumped up and down in great excitement.

She was perfectly happy about the whole situation. But I began to wonder if I was some kind of lunatic, living like a Third World refugee. No cash. No electricity. No bath.

The low point came one night after the library shut and we hiked glumly up the trail to the house with rain pouring out of the sky like crushed rock out of a dump truck. I had run out of kerosene and propane at the same time, and the firewood was damp. I put the kid to sleep and wrestled with the fire until it pinned me a third time. Then I started to cry, so I crawled into bed.

Now, remember that part of my roof that was still plastic? I kept meaning to fix it but I never did. It was like that overhead block on Bob's boat. That night it collapsed and dumped ten gallons of freezing rainwater on me. I had to crawl onto the roof with a staplegun and patch things up while the rain soaked me and the wind tried to blast me into the trees. By the time I had fixed the gaping hole I was livid. I decided that while in summer Gaia is a beautiful goddess, in winter she's a bitch. I abandoned my nuptial chamber and slept downstairs on the couch.

I didn't feel like much of a bushman by this point. I felt pathetic. Then one night a big storm blew down the hydro lines and Tofino's power was cut off for 24 hours. Me and my kid didn't even notice. I had fixed up my saw and cut a snag for firewood, and that day I remember feeling particularly cosy.

When we got into town the place was in chaos. "Hah!" I thought. "Now who's the helpless one?"

You know how when something really dangerous happens you don't start to shake till the danger has passed? A similar thing happened to me now. As the days crept slowly up out of the dark of winter, I began to see my Shadow in a whole new way.

See, I was still clinging to the hope that my Shadow was full of anger, anger I didn't want to deal with, so I kept it underground, in the unknown regions of my soul. But that didn't make sense. There was nothing unknown about my anger. After all, I was a white North American male. I'd spent years happily indulging fantasies where I macheted anyone who bugged me. Authority figures. Friends. Innocent pedestrians. I *liked* feeling angry. The thing that really disturbed me — so much that I didn't even want to know about it — was helplessness.

This cast a whole new light on my problems with women. I saw now that I had been horse-trading my Shadow. It was a simple deal: I would seek out someone who was good at being helpless, but so afraid of her anger that she'd put it in her shadow. Then we'd trade shadows. I'd be angry for her, she'd be helpless for me. No wonder I always had to be with a woman. But now I was alone out here in the forest, with no one to trade shadows with, and the helplessness was bleeding out of my shadow right before my eyes, in the form of a winter spent in the jaws of Gaia.

When this happened it was like I recovered the last piece of the circle of life. Suddenly everything looked round. It was like flying into space and seeing that the horizon, which looks like a straight line, is actually a part of an enormous ring. From that perspective, everything looked different.

I'd like to make a movie about what the world looked like as a circle; but I can't afford it. Maybe it would work as a comic book. Let's see . . . Yes, a graphic novel hosted by a strange old lady with wild hair . . . (Insert sinister old lady theme.)

FOR a long, long time there was no fish plant here, just a shoreline with some bushes and a meadow. Life was a perfect circle, and everything was dreamy. Sometimes a kid would lie down on a rock and pull a fish out of the water. But folks didn't eat fish back then. It was all catch and release. They'd look at the fish and put 'em back. In those days, the fish were perfect circles. I know it's hard to imagine circular fish, but remember — this is a comic book. Anything can happen.

The trouble began one spring morning when the surface of the water was so still folks could see their own reflections. It was a big surprise when folks first saw themselves, I tell ya. Imagine: for a couple of billion years you're running through the tall grass looking for something to eat, and something to fuck. Suddenly it's like someone holds up a mirror, and now you're watching yourself do all that.

That's when the first fish plant was built, right on the shore. Actually it was more of a temple back then, and it was all run by women, because the way stuff came out of the water reminded folks of babies being born.

These ladies had a new idea — instead of just looking at the fish, they could make chowder out of them. So they set up a net and caught all the salmon as they were swimming past the sandspit on their way to spawn. And to keep things in balance they "sacrificed" the odd fish. Chose a nice big male and lopped off its head, and threw it back in.

Those were happy times, especially if you were a woman. Every now and then some guy would ask why it always had to be a male fish that got its head bobbed, and there'd be trouble.

But that's before my time. When I got here the Ancient Greeks had had enough of the all-male-sacrifice routine, they'd kicked the women out and built a new temple.

They had a new idea: instead of waiting for the salmon to swim by, you go out on the water in a boat and catch them in a net. It was a lonely life, out there on the water, watching the horizon cut the world in half all day, but the upside was they caught so much fish they were rich in a minute. Then they had time on their hands. So they built a little clubhouse on the fish plant roof and called it head office, and they sat around inside just thinking things over.

Now, a lot of folks have a pretty formal view of the Ancient Greeks. They picture Socrates and Plato standing around in a marble hall, having a symposium. What those folks don't realize is that "symposium" is Greek for "let's get drunk together."

Now, it seems at one of these drinking parties they invented a game where you cut things in half to see how they work. It's great fun. But it's only a game. You can never understand something completely once you've cut it in half, because you lose something in the process. It's called Wholeness.

Of course, the Greeks knew this. They even had a guy called Zeno who was paid full-time just to remind them all it was only a game.

And so every evening after the fish were unloaded and packed in ice, they sat around head office, running a knife through everything in sight, just for the hell of it.

They cut the Supreme Being in half, and they called the pieces Good and Evil. They cut Sex in half, and they called the pieces Male and Female. And they ended up cutting their minds in half, and they called the pieces the Rational and the Irrational.

The Rational did all the art, and the Irrational did all the work. The Rational got a house on the hill, and the Irrational got beaten with a stick and chased into the woods. The Rational expanded head office to include a library where its perfect thoughts could live forever, and one night the Irrational showed up drunk, a cigarette got tossed in a pile of oily rags, and WOOOOMMFFF! The whole damn place went up in flames.

For a while things were pretty quiet around here. The plant was boarded up, and there was no work. Then some Romans came by on a flat barge, stripped the place down to the old foundations, and rebuilt.

Now in them days there was a young kid called Jesus who used to fish for bull heads under the dock with a piece of string and a hook.

Nice kid. A little devil at times. His life story's in the Bible. But you have to remember, the Bible was written down by fishermen. I remember it different.

Jesus had a whole new way of looking at fish. He cut them in half, the way the Greeks used to, then he tore out the guts and threw them away. Presto — nothin' but nice shiny pink meat.

So he went upstairs to put a suggestion in the suggestion box, but the million dollar view puts the zap on his brain, and he starts to babble: "I see — God is pure love. Verily, just like I done with the fish, I gotta cut the bad bit out of my soul!"

He goes out on the roof and watches the sun set. It's beautiful. As the town lights come on, he notices there's a big guy with a farmer's tan and horns sitting on a lawn chair next to him.

"Who are you?"

"You don't recognize me? I'm the animal part of your soul, which you just tried to cut out. Say, I was thinking — together, there's nothing we can't do. We could be running this outfit in a month. Think of the money. Think of the babes."

But Jesus wasn't interested. Since he got shiny and happy, all he wanted was to make the whole world shiny and happy too. So he kicked the Horned God out of head office and went downstairs to see his fishermen pals.

When they saw Christ's new soul they were amazed. It wasn't a perfect circle any more, 'cause there was a chunk missing. But so what. It sure was *shiny!* Christ figured if they came up with the right game plan, they could get the whole world to shine like that. So they brainstormed all night, and came up with an idea: they would cut the bad bit out of all the fish and use the delicious flesh to make little snacking crackers called Jesus Pieces. They wrote a little jingle:

> Je-sus Pie-ces,
> They're the Corpus Christie
> CRUNCH!

. . . And a slogan: "Mr. Christ, you make good cookies."

Then they went roaring out to sea to catch as much salmon as they could.

But what's a Horned God to do? He was kind of bummed. Rejection hurts, especially from someone as beautiful as Jesus. He slouched downstairs and asked for a job.

It was a record season. Someone had to gut all those fish. The Horned God was looking for work. Funny how things work out. Next thing you know, the Horned God has set up a cutting table and the crew's standing in a line with knives, and they're dumping the fish on the table by the hundreds and tearing out their guts with a POP! There's a big sign over the door: CUT OUT THE BAD BIT! The line was very efficient. But it was kind of grotesque. It looked like the Spanish Inquisition. First time I saw the line, I thought: "Zoiks! If fish have an afterlife, you can bet we're not the good guys."

After about a thousand years on the line, the Horned God was a nutbar. He was doing anything he could to screw up the fish. Not only that, but suddenly there weren't so many salmon around. No wonder. We were doing a million pieces a day. Severe spiritual malnutrition set in. And just when things seemed darkest, a young guy from down the shore had a great idea.

His name was Alec. He was so hot in school they called him Smart Alec. When he was just a kid he built one of those little submarines you see in the small ads at the back of *Popular Mechanics* and he used to nose around under the dock looking at the old Greek ruins down there. His new idea sounded strange at first: he said instead of just catching the fish, we should raise them ourselves. Grow 'em, like on a farm. Head office was very interested. But when he went upstairs to talk it over, the same thing happened. When he saw the view from the big desk he suddenly got a light in his eyes. "I see it all," he muttered. "God is pure reason. All we have to do is cut out the irrational part of the soul, and the earth will shine like the sun!" Next time I saw him he had really changed. He had become a fat little guy with glasses and a clipboard, and he squinted at the rest of us and introduced himself as Mr. Science.

Right then there's a knock on the plant door and in comes a kid with an Axl Rose ball cap. He claimed he was Mr. Science's bad bit — the Irrational. He wanted a desk in head office, too. "No way," says Mr. Science. "I don't know you!"

So while Mr. Science figures out what drugs to put in the fish feed, how to split the atom, and so on, the Kid is stuck down here on the line, and as the years go by he gets wilder and wilder. By the twentieth century that boy had invented drugs that could keep you smiling for a month of Sundays, and he'd stolen his uncle's notes on atom-splitting and built a bomb so big it could take out the whole plant. Then he wouldn't tell us where it was till we bought him a huge stereo. By 1961, even though there was no shortage of fish, a person never knew if they were going to make it home at night or get blown up. It was depressing.

Now, around then a woman called Venus moved to town. She was a looker. At Mardi Gras one year she rode down the street on a flatbed truck standing on a huge papier-mâché scallop shell, and every guy's tongue was hanging out a foot. She married that guy who worked for BC Tel, whose name I forget, because they had a little boy and a little girl, and after that everyone just called him Dad.

Well, Venus figured the reason everyone was so bummed at the plant was because all the decision makers up at head office were men. It didn't seem fair. So she went upstairs to fill out a complaint form.

The same damn thing happened. When she saw the gulls flocking on that distant horizon, she began to talk very quickly and with amazing precision about how God was once a woman and everything had been just perfect, but a patriarchal system of logos-based ethics had subsumed the ethnographic doohicky, then she overturned one of the desks. They said she set fire to her bra. But that can't be right. Venus never wore no bra.

So she comes back downstairs, all eloquent and fired up, and re-introduces herself as Sally. She embraced all the women as sisters, explained to the men that they were pigs, but it wasn't their fault, and said there were gonna be big changes around here. Right during her speech someone puts up her hand, a tall woman with long dark hair, and a necklace of skulls. She said her name was Kali. She suggested we just kill everyone at head office and let the Goddess sort them out.

Everyone laughed, then after the meeting Kali explained to Sally that she was her Bad Bit. Sally didn't like the idea at all. But there was no way around it. See, the kids couldn't tell the difference between the two. So Sally and Kali ended up as room mates.

After that there was all sorts of trouble at home. Venus and Dad had always fought about little stuff, like how to open pickle jars. But now Kali would pin Dad's arms while Sally pummeled him. It didn't last long after that. Around 1975 there was a nuclear family meltdown. Like a supercharged particle, Dad shot off into space.

It was hard on the kids. Now they had no male role model, just the sinister-looking black hole Dad had left when he was catapulted from their lives. There was trouble with the fish, too. At first it looked like all the male fish had tumours in them. Then Mr. Science took a look through his microscope and discovered they were actually tiny black holes. He couldn't figure out why natural selection hadn't gotten rid of the problem. Then he studied them in the hatchery, and found out the females were picking out the males with the biggest black hole.

Sally blamed Mr. Science for the black holes, and Dad for her home troubles. She might have taken a look down here, and seen what Kali was up to. But she was busy. She'd convinced head office that Jesus Pieces were passé. She had a new idea: Fish Krispies. You probably saw the commercial on Saturday mornings. You know: "They got SNAP! They got CRACKLE! But POP's never around . . ." Anyway, what with Sally's busy executive schedule and all, Kali ended up looking after the kids. And it wasn't the Brady Bunch, let me tell ya.

Girl looked like she had her shit together, then she got together

WHEN GOD WAS A WOMAN.

WHEN GOD WAS A MAN.

WHEN GOD WAS AN ANCIENT ASTRONAUT.

WHEN GOD WAS A '61 FORD THUNDERBIRD

with a lunatic who tried to rob a post office, and then held a gun to her head and demanded the cops change the words for "Happy Birthday To You" to "Now We're All Underground."

Boy was trying to figure out how to get to the Land of Dad, so to get some pointers he hung around with the Horned God and the Irrational, until one night they got in a head-on with the Old Dutch van. When they pulled Boy from the wreck there was nothing left of him but his head. It was pathetic, I tell ya. Kali would bring him to work in a brown paper bag, and set him on the table while she ate her sandwich. Boy talked about his plans to visit Dad some day. Kali would just laugh.

"Forget it. You're going to stay with me, and skateboard and party till you die."

Back when Kali was part of Venus, that laugh was the neatest thing about her. Ten years on the line, and it was sounding downright sinister.

So just a few years back this woman called Gaia who lives on an island across from the spit and grows organic veggies in a plastic teepee shows up, enraged about the black holes in the fish she was catching. She said it was because the fish plant was dumping all its waste right back into the collective unconscious. She storms up to head office with a list of demands, and the same damn thing happens all over again.

There's a flash of light, and instead of Gaia there's this pretty young thing called Mother Nature standing there, lovely as Meares Island in midsummer. She comes back downstairs all epiphanied, with flowers in her hair and a placard that says: "Me First!" And she waxes lyrical about how she's going to save the natural world from man's ruthless domination. God is a woman. The earth is our mother. This patriarchal culture has been trashing nature for too long, and it's got to stop. Nature is good. Nature is nice. Flowers. Seal pups. Paradise.

Sally gives her the thumbs up from the top of the stairs. Then there's a cough at the back, and old Mrs. Winters, who had suddenly appeared by the wash tank, but seemed to have always been there, rumbles: "What about smallpox? I heard on TV how there's only a few of the little buggers left, frozen solid in a jar in a research institute in the States. I sure hope you're gonna lobby to protect that species, cause it's in a lotta trouble."

Mother Nature shakes her head.

"How come?" rumbles old Mrs. Winters. "It's a hunnert percent natural, ain't it?"

For a moment Mother Nature was at a loss. Then she said: "Well . . . I was going to start by getting organic coffee in the lunchroom."

Mrs. Winters laughed. "It don't matter how clean them beans are, when they travel ten thousand miles to your cup, it's 'Game over, Gaia.' "

Big laughs from the crew.

Mrs. Winters goes on: "There's nothing unnatural about hating nature, bub. Nature is like a beautiful lady who says, 'I might make love to you, or I might kill you and eat you.' Everyone hates nature, it's just that some folks are up front about it."

Right then the Horned God showed up with another tote full of fish, and we had to get back to work. Mother Nature disappeared upstairs and got to work making the world more female. Old Mrs. Winters has been driving the hundred clicks from Port every morning, and she's gone a little bananas, what with the Clive Cussler novels and all. Every day she brings a huge Pharmasave bottle of estrogen and dumps it in the wash tank when no one's watching. Maybe that's why the fish have started to grow breasts. Even the jacks. Frankly, I'm concerned. But Old Mrs. Winters, she just laughs that dry rumble of a laugh you get from working on the line too long, and now and then she picks up a buxom bottomfeeder and shakes it at the steps that lead up to head office. "Is that female enough for you?" she growls.

Y'know . . . it's times like this I almost feel like explaining what the hell's been going on these past two thousand years. It's all so simple:

when you walk towards a light, your shadow gets bigger. That's why I like to find a bit of middle ground. But what do I know? I'm just the old lady who washes the gloves.

— The End —

Okay, okay, so it's not the history of the world, it's just me again, projecting on a grand scale. It's as plain as the gnosis on my faceis.

But I no longer saw projection as a bad habit that was going to make hair grow on the palms of my soul. When I began to see things in circles I saw projection as a circle, too. A sort of heroic journey: a part of my soul, ready to become conscious, ventures forth into the world, and meets with someone that resembles it. There's a clash between the projection and the real thing. Then the projection is welcomed home, and there's a big celebration, because the soul is now more conscious.

That's the theory. Unfortunately, what usually happens to me is when the projection comes home I welcome it if it's shiny and happy, but if it's the Hitler in me, I lock the door.

I wasn't sure how to welcome home those extremely naughty parts of me back into my soul yet — but the circular view of life gave me great peace of mind. I put down the heavy load of trying to make the world a better place. But Loud Sue's insights also led me into a bit of a backwater. I mean, if everything was a circle, what was the point of going anywhere or doing anything? As spring approached, I figured I'd spend the whole sunny season alone at my house watching the trees grow.

Just goes to show how wrong you can be.

CHAPTER SEVEN

Spring

ONCE every seven years or so, the warm El Niño current hits town, like an eccentric uncle who's been researching hallucinogenic plants in the Amazon, then shows up at your door one spring evening, laden with tales from the tropics.

The water gets toasty warm. Rumours fly: sharks spotted off Lovekin Rock. Crab pots full of exotic flora. Salmon smolt nuked by mackerel . . . It's an El Niño summer.

Such summers are tinged with magic. The last time the El Niño came to town I ended up travelling to Tibet. And this time something even stranger happened.

It started innocently enough. I struck up a friendship with a young woman called River who had come up from Vancouver to help the Friends rescue the rainforest.

The first time I saw her I thought she was lovely. She looked just like my Anima did in that dream where the city lit up.

One night she invited me to her place for tea. At this point I knew nothing about her except that she drew spirals on everything and smoked like a little blonde chimney. But I suspected she might be an ecofeminist witch.

Anyway, we went to her little cabin on the inlet. It was cool: dried flowers, bundles of kindling, and a shrine over the bed made from moss, bones, and twigs, with a big abalone shell for burning sage in. She also had all those books: *When God Was a Woman. The Beauty Myth. The Chalice and the Sword.*

We started off with a great discussion about magic, but sadly this led into a huge fight over whether or not men had trashed the planet. I said human destruction might have a man's face on the label, but if you checked the ingredients, they were 50 percent female. The evening went downhill from there.

During the spring we had the odd chat, and though I thought she was very interesting, we didn't seem to have much in common. And anyway, I was spending all my time in the forest.

Up at my dream house things were going well. When the good weather hit I finally tore down the plastic over my bed and fixed the roof. Now my bed looked great. It stuck out one side of the house so that it was surrounded by trees. There were going to be windows around it soon, but that spring the walls were open. When I lay on it, I felt like I was floating high up in the forest canopy. Steller's jays landed on the foot of my bed in the morning. Raccoons came and sat on the window ledge. I decided to keep it open until the fall.

I'd always known in my head that winter yields to spring; that year I had felt it in my belly. Lately I felt everything in my belly. Since childhood I'd protected my belly with a healthy padding of fat. I guess it was Head Office's way of controlling the emotional chaos down there. But these days Head Office had dwindled to the status of a provincial weather station; and my belly dwindled also, until one day I looked sideways in the mirror and decided it could no longer be described as big and soft. And the more I carried supplies up my trail, the leaner I became. I chopped wood. I carried groceries. I lay on my bed and stared at the forest for hours, marvelling at how beautiful Gaia looked when she wasn't trying to kill me. Going a round with her on her own terms had made me feel very differently about Gaia. Back when I got arrested I had thought I loved her. And I did — so long as I had her pinned to the mat. But it wasn't really love.

This felt more real. I lay there for hours. Days. Weeks. It was better than MuchMusic. Then one afternoon a chevron of geese flew low over the house, honking in the blue heavens. It was like an arrow shot from my belly up into my heart. Winter seemed like a dream. Spring had come inside and outside my body.

One part of me was still trapped in winter: my face. At this point I had a flaming red beard, down to my chest. Older guys were always praising my mondo beard. I didn't want to give it up. But I didn't want my face to be trapped in winter, either. So one morning I took a Stanley utility knife and hacked it off. Then I shaved. When I looked in the mirror I had lost ten years. I hardly knew myself. "Anything could happen to that person," I thought.

My beard had concealed my emotions well, mushing them all together into a steady patriarchal grouchiness. Now my emotions were exposed. My face had caught up with my belly. I was delighted. I decided to go down to town and surprise my friends.

When I got to the post office I bumped into River. She had never seen me without a beard. She beamed up at me and said, "Andrew — you're cute!"

I was utterly surprised. I don't feel very cute. There's something very Spam about the shape of my head. And like the ozone, the hair over my personal north pole is getting dangerously thin. To cover my discomfort (which now showed on my face), I thought I had better make some wise-ass remark. My mouth wagged open but nothing came out. River continued to beam up at me. I began to blush. I backed away from her, nodding and grinning like a big Chinese hand puppet. I felt like a jackass — but I decided I liked River a lot.

Around then my X-Wife hired River to babysit. One evening she dropped my daughter off at my dream house. My daughter was crazy about her, and she ended up staying for supper. Things were going well until my kid began to sing her favourite song, "Terriers", by the Kids in the Hall. You know: "Nobody wants to die/But everybody dies/Dies. Dies. Dies! Dies!/Worms eating your — eyes."

River looked a little freaked. "This is what I get for not repressing my daughter's dark side," I thought. She looked like a little red-haired Kali. But after the kid was asleep, River said she thought it was "neat" that I let my daughter talk about death and worms. She'd only been allowed to feel happy, shiny thoughts when she was little. Now she wanted to reclaim that dark Kali power; that's why she wanted to go to the Kennedy Bridge protest camp and battle the patriarchy. She thought it would empower her and at the same time wake something in the loggers that they had been robbed of: their gentleness.

When she put it that way, I found it hard to shoot her down. Instead, I told her my theory about how men and women had traded shadows, and all the trouble I'd had getting back my gentleness.

We sat by the stove and polished off a bottle of wine, and a whole new picture of River emerged: a wild salmon, born in the urban fish farm, she had escaped the city and what she called "the hot pursuit of happiness". Now she wanted to live gently off the earth, leave as small a wake as possible. So she worked at the organic store in exchange for veggies and babysat her landlady's grandkid in exchange for her cabin. She only needed a little cash for tobacco. I was impressed. We ended up talking for hours.

When she left, we hugged. Our bellies met. There was a weird rumble. She giggled. "Our bellies like each other," she said.

A few days later, she came for supper again. We smoked a hundred cigarettes and talked about the Shadow, Kali, and the animal magic of the Horned God.

I knew she loved spirals, so I told her about the Fibonacci numbers: 1, 1, 2, 3, 5, 8, 13, 21, 34, 55, 89, 144, 233, 377, 610, and so on. You get these numbers by adding the last two: 1+1=2, 1+2=3, 2+3=5,

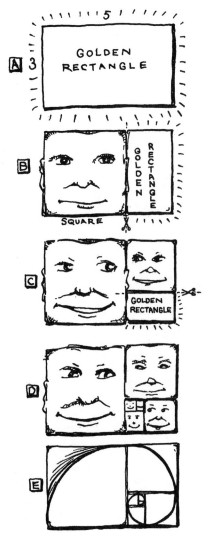

3+5=8, 5+8=13, and so on, til you run out of paper. Now, the ratio of each number to the next — 3:5, 5:8, 8:13 and so on — is called the Golden Ratio, and a rectangle with Fibonacci numbers for sides is what the Ancient Greeks called a Golden Rectangle — the most beautiful rectangle in the world. A lot of old buildings, like the Acropolis, are based on golden rectangles. Where do the spirals come in?

Oh, right . . .

Draw a golden rectangle. A: Cut off a square. B: The leftover piece is also a golden rectangle. Cut a square off of it, too. C: You get a third golden rectangle. Keep going until there's no more room inside. D: Now draw a line connecting the cut-off points. E: Hey, it's a spiral! Even more curious, certain plants always have a Fibonacci number of seeds. Sunflowers, for example, have either 89 or 144 seeds. Some huge ones have 254 seeds. It's like a marriage between vegetables and mathematics, and the nuptial chamber is the spiral, the pattern found in storms and conch shells.

Immediately River wanted to cut an apple in half and see if it was true. Suddenly, I was afraid. I'd never actually looked. What if it was all bunk? But it was too late to start making retractions. We got an apple and cut it in two, and to my relief there were five seed pockets. Not only that, they looked like a little pentacle.

After that we got into all sorts of stuff: palindromes, anagrams, mystic numbers . . . It was the middle of the night before I knew it.

Another hundred cigarettes, a quiet talk by candlelight, and she crashed on my couch.

River was beautiful. She had that natural gazelle beauty that can't be faked. She even looked beautiful when she was screwing up her face to get something out of her eye.

But I didn't want to fall in love. For me, falling in love is like going over Niagara Falls in a testosterone barrel. I was finally happy with my own company, and I wanted to keep it that way. I knew if I fell in love,

I'd do what I always do: confuse River with my Anima, begin to think she was a part of my soul, freak out at the idea that she might leave, cling to her like a drowning man, and so on . . . No, we were better off as friends. So the summer grew rich and green around us; we explored the inlet in her green canoe; we smoked a million Drum cigarettes; we ate only organic veggies; then late one evening, just as naturally as spring follows winter, our faces finally caught up with our bellies, and we began to kiss.

A few days later, it was time for River to battle the patriarchy. I thought it was a little rough on the loggers to drag them into this new-age 'Nam, but I was determined to help River bring Kali out into the light. So I borrowed a car to drop her off at the Kennedy Bridge protest camp. I vowed not to get involved this time — to stay aloof.

The camp was in an old clearcut. It looked like the valley where the dinosaurs had gone extinct, with great bleached stumps twisting into the sky and a dry, hot wind flapping the kitchen tent. I kissed River goodbye, leaped into the car, gunned the engine, and roared into a ditch. I flailed about — reverse, first, reverse, first — until the Friends gathered around and rocked me back onto the road, waving and smiling in their eco-friendly way. So aloof.

On the long drive back into town, I pondered our strange role reversal: River was going into battle; I was going home to look after my kid. I had to smile. Our romance had been fun, but I was pretty sure we'd reached the last page. Blockades are very intense, and a lot of people mistake the adrenaline for love. I could see it now: River would meet some eco-warrior on the bridge. Someone her own age. Someone with hair. Well, so be it.

A few days later, River lay down on Kennedy Bridge surrounded by flowers and magic spells and got hauled away while loggers cursed and cameras rolled and her eco-buddies sang "I am a wise woman/I am a healing woman" in the background. I heard the whole story at the organic food store. "Wow," I thought, "the ultimate volcano virgin."

When she got back to town, she was totally empowered and radiant. She looked like Barbie and Buddha's love-child. I was in over my head. But I came up with a plan: I asked River if she wanted to canoe with me up to the Megin — that virgin river valley beyond Sulphur Pass that I'd set out to protect so long ago but had never actually seen.

She said yes, so one morning in August we loaded up her canoe with supplies and paddled off into the wilderness. When we reached the Atleo clearcut we stopped for lunch. I made a cashew butter sandwich, she cut off her long blonde hair and buried it under a stump. Then we paddled up Miller Channel past the old protest camp and on, to the Megin.

Now if you're thinking that paddling into paradise with a woman you're trying not to fall in love with is a crazy plan, you're right. It's almost like my Irrational thought it up. It didn't work at all. As soon as all traces of civilization had vanished behind us, the Horned God, locked away for eons in the base of my spine, roused from his ancient slumber. It was just like I'd always hoped would happen with Orange Ted on those long car journeys: River held some food up to my mouth, and I woke up to eat.

By the time we got back to town the jig was up. We were in love. I'd been in love before, but this was different. It was like a mixture of Eden before the Fall and Hiroshima after the Bomb. Some days we wandered around in the forest eating and making love and talking in whispers; other days we shouted at each other and stormed off to our respective homes, never to cross paths again. It was rocky at first, but soon we got good at fighting. The key to good fighting was having our own places. So long as I had an Inner Sanctum where I could go alone, a place where the most monstrous part of me could feel at home, I felt I could share the rest of myself freely.

That fall when River went down to court for stopping the logging at Kennedy Bridge, I went with her and the rest of the Friends.

It's hard to describe the strange mutation the Friends had gone through. Maybe we should trade places again, like we did at the fish plant . . . (Insert sinister new-age mood music.)

Evening. Autumnal solstice. You duck under a driftwood arch into the garden, and there they are: the Friends. Things sure have changed since Sulphur Pass days. The Friends now see things from an ecofeminist perspective, they show videos like *The Burning Times*, and they sponsor Unlearning Racism workshops at which men are not allowed.

The new skipper is Helen, longtime Tofino resident and overly concerned citizen. For years she was homeless, just like you. She desperately wanted a house, a safe haven from which to battle the patriarchy. But rental accommodation in Tofino is scarce, and she couldn't find anything. Then one day her dad showed up, plunked down 200 thou, and bought the property next to Poole's land, which has not one but three houses on it. Her homeless days were over.

Then there's Garp, a hyper-activist wildlife photographer, a man so full o' beans it looks like he's being worked from above with strings.

And Hilda. Can she ever sing! She can hit notes that usually only a squeegee can reach.

And Morag, whose family fuse goes off every time she even gets close to a logging truck. Ironically, you once helped deliver a truckload of huge cedar beams to the mondo house she was building on Chestermans Beach. That was one truck that escaped her wrath.

And Starface. She feels compelled to talk for the trees, compelled to explain what Susan Faludi is all about, compelled to tell you what she had for lunch, compelled to explain why she changed direction halfway across the room . . .

And Amos'n'Andi, the eco-warrior couple. They eat only organic food. Once you offered them some organic chocolate, but they declined because it had milk solids in it. "We're organic *vegans*," they explained sadly.

And Isis, the WASP giantess. An imposing figure: huge white hands with very red knuckles, horn-rimmed glasses and a pale floral print dress. Her back is so big the floral print looks like wallpaper. She spent the summer down on Hornby Island, reiki-ing in the cash; now she's in Tough City to lead a witchy ritual and get the Goddess on side for the trial in Supreme Court in Victoria.

You're looking forward to the ritual, because you heard there's a part where they welcome the Horned God. So you blast into the circle with all your dark male energy, but an arch glance from the WASP giantess convinces you you should have checked your horns at the door.

The ritual is great. Now your roots go down, down into the earth. And hey, your horns will grow back. A few days later, at 4 a.m., a bunch of you pack into a huge twelve-seater van with Amos the vegan pagan at the helm. His plan: drop you off in Victoria, then blast this fossil-fuel starship back up to Tough City because that night there's a benefit dinner for the organic food store. Fortunately for Gaia, the wheel comes off the starship just as you pull in to town.

When you get to court the crowd is divided into two teams: loggers on one side of the courtroom, environmentalists on the other, and a wide swath of DMZ seating down the centre. You sit in the DMZ and frolic with your girlfriend until the bailiff tells you to stop.

First up to bat is Morag. She makes a long and impassioned speech about logging trucks and hypocrisy, then you all break for lunch. You stand in a circle with the rest of the crew in the cathedral grounds across from the courthouse, listening to Morag rail against Y chromosomes. You are determined not to take out the psychic garbage this time. Instead of rashly mentioning the beams in Morag's monster house you visualize all the sushi you're going to eat for lunch. Suddenly someone says, "Hey — we're standing on the path and there's nice grass right next to us!"

ZAP! The circle is broken as ten pairs of Birkenstocks leap for the lawn. It's an electroshock consensus decision. Suddenly, you stand alone. It's a tense moment. If you leap for the grass you'll be conforming. If you don't you'll be rebelling. All you really want to do is go for sushi. So you blurt out, "I'm going for sushi," and everyone looks bewildered.

The sushi is delicious, but the rest of the trial is a skid mark of legalese, eagle feathers and coffee breaks. The judge taps his mondo desk with a pencil and thinks about snow tires; the eco-warriors claim a purity of motive that should put them above the law — or at least to one side of it — and go on and on about trees and ozone and Gandhi until His Lordship snaps and cries, "But we have to have Rule of Law or we'll have chaos!" Meanwhile, every turnip patch in the Baltic is ready to trade A-bombs for sandwiches. You wonder glumly what chaos is going to look like when it finally arrives.

Three days and thirty thousand tax-dollars later, BAM! Down comes the gavel. Everyone gets twenty days of electronic monitoring and immediately begins to complain that electromagnetic radiation is shooting out of their mandatory jewellery into their ankles and creating a health hazard. The state just can't avoid oppressing some folks. But anyway, you get the picture. We can trade back now.

When River went up to bat I was pretty nervous. She had no lawyer because she thought that would just tangle her in a patriarchal war metaphor. She took her spell bag and her eagle feather and sort of tiptoed up to the judge's desk, surrounded by magic.

Pretty soon the Crown ran into trouble. River's whole arrest had been videotaped, but the tape was lost. Not only that, but the Friends' lawyer took a major Anima shine to her and was able to prove (free of charge) that she'd been arrested on a badly worded injunction. It took the judge, the Friends' lawyer, and the prosecution about two minutes to agree: then BAM! Down came the gavel. River was free. "Wow," I thought, "ecofeminist witch kicks patriarchal ass!"

By the time we got back to the Sound, River and I were bonded like Brinks guards, paired like wild salmon, bestowed, smitten, and

real, real gone. Maybe it was the adrenaline. Who knows? All I know is, I wanted to spend the rest of my life getting to know this mysterious woman. I wanted to be with her until the Atleo clearcut was a stand of giant cedars once more, and raise hippie children with her on some faraway beach.

Before we settled down for the rest of eternity, River wanted to go on a big adventure to Scotland to discover her roots. Now, to me, Scotland is about as exciting as Burnaby. I don't see tartan, hills and castles, I see bus stops, TV, and those bleak electric fireplaces with plastic coal. But love is an amazing thing. Suddenly the bagpipes in my heart began to play, and I wanted to go too. Rent a cottage in the highlands. Spend the summer in the land of my birth. It sounded very romantic. So we began to plan a journey to the old country: she would leave in the spring. I would go fishing with Peter on the *Dawn*, and we would meet in Scotland in a couple of months.

That winter I tried working at the fish plant. Not much had changed down there, except there was a blood-spattered boom box hanging on a nail, so now you could hear Sarah McLachlan's dulcet tones mixed in with the roar of the fishgut grinder. I stuck to it for a bit. But it really bummed me out when I'd come staggering home from hell, rattling and reeking like thirty half-used tins of salmon cat chow, and River would whimper and crawl to the far end of the futon without even waking up. After two months I quit, and for the rest of the winter River and I lay by the wood stove with our legs entwined, smoked cigarettes, and talked about hiking in the highlands of Scotland.

We were broke. We wore rags. We ate berries off bushes. We didn't care. We spent a lot of time staring into each others' eyes. My roof leaked, and I didn't fix it. I didn't have to, because I ended up hanging out at River's little cabin a lot. Then one night as we lay crashed on her futon, I had a very strange dream . . .

I dreamt I was driving alongside the Fraser River up near Prince George. There was a baby in a booster seat next to me. I looked like a young James Garner, with a fleece-lined leather jacket like he wore in *The Great Escape*. Suddenly the car went off the road and plunged into the river. Before I could get the door open I had to solve a series of mathematical equations on a little chalkboard. I had just enough time to solve them all, provided I stayed completely calm and ignored the terror welling up inside me. At last I got the math done, the door opened, and I slid out of the car. Then I remembered the . . . puppy. Yeah, that's right — the puppy on the passenger's seat. I realized sadly that there was no time to go back for him. So sad. Oh well, it was only a puppy. Anyway, he was asleep, snuffling like he was chasing rabbits in a dream. Shh. Better let him sleep . . . But as I rose through the water the snuffling became a whimper, a moan, a scream, and a voice cried out: "IT'S NOT A PUPPY! IT'S A BABY!!!"

I crawled onto the bank and stood there shivering. I felt totally spooked. I could still hear the baby crying down there in the cold, dark water. There was no way to get back down to the car. There was a city in the distance, so I hitched there. The first guy I ran into was big Leo. He was drunk, and he had a weird metal helmet thing on his head with keys dangling from the chin guard. "Well, they've finally done it," he slurred proudly. "Invented a machine that can cut a thousand trees a second."

As he spoke, this *thing* lumbered into view behind him. It was massive, like a building-sized woodstove on tank treads, and it was cutting the trees from whole hillsides with a single slash.

"But how long will it take till the whole sound is cut?" I asked. Leo shrugged, "Twenty minutes?"

I was horrified. No more trees. No more jobs. This was the end of everything. Leo agreed. "End of everything," he slurred. "And the best part is — it doesn't even *use* the fucking trees. Just *burns* 'em . . ."

When I woke up I told River my dream, and said, "I've got to get that baby out of that car." "Or maybe you have to let it go," she said. It turned out we were both right.

That Christmas we were so broke we gave each other a book about tantric lore. Part of the book was about the chakras: seven power points in the human body. It was very interesting. At that time I knew nothing of this stuff — to me, Kundalini sounded like an Asian pasta dish. But when I started reading, I found to my amazement that my whole adventure since Sulphur Pass mirrored a descent through the main chakras. Here's a drawing:

I was blown away. I was a little miffed at first that everything I'd discovered on my great solo voyage around the poles of existence was common knowledge to a billion or so Third World peasants. But the upside was, it looked like I was in tune with the cosmos after all.

There was only one chakra to go: the Root Chakra, which looked pretty scary. It was where the primal energy of the circle of life, the Kundalini, hung out, in the form of a serpent. From it all creative energy flowed up the spine and into this universe.

The Root Chakra covered creation, regeneration, and birth — but also elimination, destruction, death, and letting go — all the bad bits of the circle of life. In the body, the bad bit of this ominous chakra manifested itself as the anus. I began to wonder how it would manifest itself in my life.

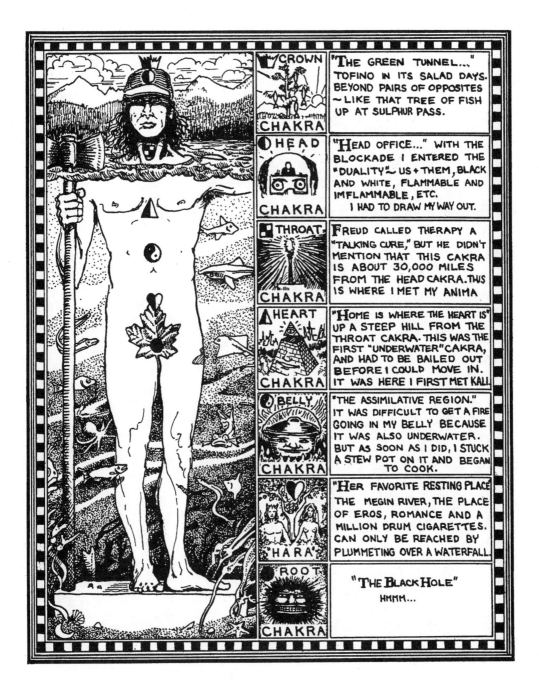

CROWN CHAKRA

"THE GREEN TUNNEL..." TOFINO IN ITS SALAD DAYS. BEYOND PAIRS OF OPPOSITES ~ LIKE THAT TREE OF FISH UP AT SULPHUR PASS.

HEAD CHAKRA

"HEAD OFFICE..." WITH THE BLOCKADE I ENTERED THE "DUALITY"~ US + THEM, BLACK AND WHITE, FLAMMABLE AND IMFLAMMABLE, ETC.
I HAD TO DRAW MY WAY OUT.

THROAT CHAKRA

FREUD CALLED THERAPY A "TALKING CURE," BUT HE DIDN'T MENTION THAT THIS CAKRA IS ABOUT 30,000 MILES FROM THE HEAD CAKRA. THIS IS WHERE I MET MY ANIMA

HEART CHAKRA

"HOME IS WHERE THE HEART IS" UP A STEEP HILL FROM THE THROAT CAKRA. THIS WAS THE FIRST "UNDERWATER" CAKRA, AND HAD TO BE BAILED OUT BEFORE I COULD MOVE IN. IT WAS HERE I FIRST MET KALI.

BELLY CHAKRA

"THE ASSIMILATIVE REGION." IT WAS DIFFICULT TO GET A FIRE GOING IN MY BELLY BECAUSE IT WAS ALSO UNDERWATER. BUT AS SOON AS I DID, I STUCK A STEW POT ON IT AND BEGAN TO COOK.

"HARA"

"HER FAVORITE RESTING PLACE THE MEGIN RIVER, THE PLACE OF EROS, ROMANCE AND A MILLION DRUM CIGARETTES. CAN ONLY BE REACHED BY PLUMMETING OVER A WATERFALL.

ROOT CHAKRA

"THE BLACK HOLE" HMMM...

Black Hole Summer

SPRING got off to an odd start when my cat crawled into our bed during a big storm and popped three kittens. The first two were skookum; the third had something wrong with its neck. The cat took one look at number three and crunched its head. Then she lay there, breast-feeding two of her babies and eating the third, purring as she tore its flesh off in strips. Worship of Kali came naturally to my cat. But I found the whole scene hard to take. How on earth was I supposed to live life like a perfect circle when the bad bit was so *bad*? I mean, eating my young is a little out of my league.

Not long after that, River set out on her journey. On our last morning together, I woke early so I could watch her face while she slept. This was going to hurt. It's one thing to let go of your lover once you've spiraled into hatred. But how do you let go in midsummer?

I figured it would be good practice for letting go of other things in life, such as teeth and hair. Also, it was a chance to prove to myself that I hadn't confused River with my Anima. And anyway, it was only for a few months. A few hours later, we kissed good-bye and told each other we'd meet again in Scotland. And off she went.

Meanwhile, the Battle for Clayoquot Sound was heating up. The Friends had begun to get big-time support. Everyone from Ecotrust to Greenpeace was suddenly on the bandwagon. The green standard was raised against the spring sky, looking considerably less shoddy than it had the year before, when it had been made from an old sheet.

The opposition, everyone from Mac Blo to the Reverend Sun Myung Moon, finally got its shit together and chose a colour (yellow) and a team name (Share BC). They explained that they wanted to "share" the trees. Smacks of Barney, doesn't it? I'm well-acquainted with this kind of sharing from playing with my five-year-old. Basically, the yellow team wanted to cut down the trees and *then* share them.

Now, the loggers out here are a tough bunch. It's hard to get them to wear ribbons — let alone yellow ribbons. But a war metaphor is a war metaphor. Pretty soon, yellow ribbons were streaming from half the car antennas in town.

To calm these troubled waters, Premier Mike told everyone that on April 13th he would unveil a plan that would make everybody happy. On the big day, he flew up here and drove to the summit of Radar Hill, where he gazed through Coke-bottle glasses at the worthless, scrubby shore pines that swept down to the ocean, and pronounced: "Trees as far as the eye can see."

He didn't look much like a patriarch. He reminded me more of my Uncle Archie, who took me to the movies on Saturdays and always hurt his back by leaping down the theatre steps three at a time to impress me.

When he revealed his plan, there was a deathly hush. He'd tried to placate both teams by taking away huge tracts of timber from the yellows and offering the greens a vision of the wilderness that was disturbingly reminiscent of a government office: cramped little cubbyholes of old growth connected by narrow corridors of trees. Suddenly it became apparent that Uncle Mike had been stuck in head office for way too long. At once, the greens and the yellows saw red. Battle lines were drawn. And the Black Hole Summer began.

For the kickoff Paul Watson showed up in his big black boat the *Sea Shepherd* and fired off his cannon. Nobody in town was impressed — it brought to mind the time the English sailed up here and shelled Opitsat, the Native village across the harbour.

In June, Tofino's town council had to vote on whether to review logging practices within Clayoquot Sound or to go ahead with business as usual. One councillor, a local crab fisherman, voted for business as usual. That night his boat, the *Clayoquot Isle*, mysteriously burst into flames. Next day, the headline of the *Province* screamed "BURNING HATE". This did little to resolve the tension in town. The green team said it was an insurance scam. Right. Like you'd burn your own boat and then appear on the cover of the *Province* the next day yelling about arson. The yellow team said it was ecoterrorism. Well, I don't know — but I do know that three of my pals were partying pretty good on the *Clayoquot Isle* that night. Beer. Cigarettes. Who can say?

Anyway, what really bugged me about the whole thing was this: I loved that boat. It used to be my pal Leo's boat. That first summer, when I was young and broke, Leo bought me some food and got me to paint the name on the prow. Now another piece of old Tofino was gone, and nobody mourned its passing; everyone was too busy fighting over who was to blame.

When July rolled around, the Friends set up a Peace Camp in the Black Hole clearcut. Peace Camp. What a joke! Like a concentration camp is a place you go to concentrate.

Running the show was a woman named Tzapata. She was from Toronto. I met her a few times but didn't get a clear impression of her, because she moved so fast her features were a blur in my head. All I remembered was that she had long red hair and a degree in something like ecofeminism. She ran the Black Hole on ecofeminist principles, explaining to the *Globe and Mail* that women were more in touch with the Earth, so they should make the ecological decisions. It's sort of like saying that men are more in touch with the banks, so they should make the financial decisions.

Tzapata was right when she complained that all the decisions, from which valley to destroy right down to where to park the crummy, were made by men, but she skipped over the fact that all these men were raised by women. If the women of the world made such a mess of the boys, wouldn't that be reflected in how they handled the Earth? Just a thought.

The media circus really began when Midnight Oil offered to do a benefit concert for Clayoquot Sound. As the big day approached, camera crews amassed like blackflies and our little town struggled like a virgin on the altar of mass media. The biggest yacht any of us had ever seen was anchored in the harbour. Rumours flew. Neil Young was on board. Arnold Schwarzenegger was on board. Half of Hollywood was on board. The locals fell under a dark enchantment. Suddenly every blonde at the bakery was Sharon Stone; Richard Gere and the Dalai Lama were headed here on foot.

At first I was untouched by this spell. I'm not big in the fan department. I like to be the star of my own life. Then, on the morning before the concert, I walked into town and ran into Kim, who told me the singer from the Tragically Hip was staying at Morag's mondo bed-and-breakfast out on Chestermans Beach. Great. The one celebrity I'd be starstruck meeting. I decided to get a burrito, but when I got to the burrito joint there was a guy sitting outside who looked like the Hip's vocalist. I wandered away, overcome with shyness. Then I ran into Joe, who told me Midnight Oil had just pulled in at the dock.

Hip behind me, Oil before me — I felt like the filling in a rock-star sandwich. I headed up my trail and hung out at my house for three days, hoping things would cool down.

Midnight Oil had originally planned to play at Kennedy Bridge, where River got arrested. They hoped to get 5,000 rockers to block the road. Greenpeace had already built a stage. But the night before the concert, the local Native council decided this spectacle was distracting folks from their own struggle for aboriginal rights. They asked everyone to leave Kennedy Bridge, which was their ancestors' land. So Greenpeace had to tear down the stage during the night and rebuild it out at the Black Hole. Hmm — Big multinational from Down Under punches a hole in the rainforest. Big rock group from Down Under appears in the hole, singing their antipodean lungs out. Some kind of yin/yang thing there.

August was a patchwork of Fellini outtakes. Robert "No Bobs on a Dead Planet" Kennedy zoomed up from the States and appeared in the papers being carried ashore in a canoe by all the local Native chiefs like some weird whitebread pharoah.

Tom Hayden of the Chicago Seven got married on the beach at Chetarpe. During the vows he promised to protect Clayoquot Sound and its natural wonders. My pal Crabber Dave played the mandolin for the wedding party. He said folks were grossed out when he cleaned a salmon in front of them. I guess fishguts are natural, but not wonderful.

Out at the junction the Black Hole was filled with a galaxy of stars. Neo-pagan witches like Starhawk brought their wisdom into the fray. Men of the cloth, who under normal circumstances might have been denounced by the Friends as patriarchal pederasts, were on-side. Child troubadour Raffi sang outside the local jail. It was a new-age *Gong Show*.

Like a lot of locals, I tried to stay out of the line of fire. But there was no refuge from the war metaphor. Every time I turned on a TV there was some 60-year-old logger from down the road talking in sound bites. Not even our Sunday night coffeehouse was sacred. Once, the local musicians just got together in the room over the pub and rocked out with tunes like "White Wedding" and "Orange Blossom Special". Now we had to sit there while Morag read long, clunky poems about how the Earth was our mother and loggers were rapists. By the time the smoke cleared about 700 people had been arrested. The Friends, who the

winter before had asked me for ten bucks to help cover the office hydro bill, had blown a hundred grand.

Summer faded. The face of Mother Winter appeared in the sky over the Black Hole. Things got tense. Tzapata got in a giant queen-bee struggle with Artemis, a woman who had been with the Friends since Sulphur Pass days. Artemis got fired. When The Boss can tell you to clean out your desk, it's just not anarchy any more. The Friends were no longer *coup* . . . they were *d'état*.

At last, winter came. The denizens of the Black Hole fled to the city: hot showers, pasta Alfredo, and videos. But the dregs at the bottom, who'd been battening on the free macrobiotic food all summer, now picked themselves up, staggered into town, and showed up at Poole's Land asking for sanctuary.

Things had changed in the two years I'd been on the Land. About 100 people had tried to join the commune. The shiny, happy side of Poole (which could not say no) welcomed every one of them. Delighted, his new converts would throw together a temporary structure and begin work on something more permanent. But then the shadow side of Poole would sneak up on them from behind and bite them so badly they'd leave in a huff. By that fall, the front of the Land was a warren of half-finished tent platforms. Poole himself was mystified by the whole dynamic, because he and his shadow lived on different continents, and could only communicate by satellite.

When the remnants of the Black Hole showed up the situation was particularly sensitive. That very week town council, on behalf of Poole's neighbours, was considering enacting a bylaw that would give it the power to tear down all the structures on the Land that were not up to code.

Poole's shiny, happy side begged the Black Hole crew not to stay in his usual way. "Welcome, comrades!" he said. Soon there was a huge plastic tent-thing right by the road with about 30 deadbeats drumming and showering and shitting in buckets. Town got wind of it and the bylaw was passed. Everything on the Land that was not to code had to go. Suddenly my dream house was slated for destruction.

I hadn't paid much attention to the Land's problems because I'd been busy with my own. Despite my theories about my Anima and my desire to be whole on my own, I found that when River left, I had a Black Hole inside me the size of Jupiter.

After she left, the sun got hot and the days grew long, but it didn't feel like summer. I dealt with my pain in the traditional way: I ignored it. But it loomed over me like a thunder cloud.

The months passed, and my Kundalini sauce got backed up pretty good. By solstice things began to get weird. On the shortest night of the year I dreamt I was looking for a little kid who was lost in the woods. I crawled around in my sleep until I fell out of bed. Normally this would not be a big deal; but remember, my bed "floated high up in the forest canopy." I plummeted twenty feet down the side of my house and landed on two plate glass windows I'd carried up the trail the day before. They were supposed to be around my bed.

Miraculously I wasn't killed, but I woke up in shock, pitch darkness, and total pain, gushing blood in all directions. The entire right side of my body was a mass of cuts and bruises. I wrapped a sheet around my leg and waited till dawn; then I hobbled to Leo's house, where I washed up.

That same morning, Peter, my skipper, handed the helm of the *Dawn* over to his new deckhand and the young chucklehead hit the rock off the beach below my house. The boat sprung a plank, and Peter had to run her up onto the beach. The whole thing unnerved him, and he decided not to go trolling for sockeye. Now I had to find money for my trip to Scotland elsewhere.

When I survived my nocturnal plunge I figured I'd passed through the Black Hole by cheating death. But it wasn't so. That was an *hors d'oeuvres*. The main course didn't show up till August. I can't tell you about the strange adventure I went on that month because it was an Inner Sanctum thing, and not only that, but in this Root Chakra the

Black Hole seems to suck everything in that gets close, like a black hole in physics. It's the most dangerous part of the journey. But around that time I stumbled on an ancient myth that summed up what I went through.

It's the story of the Fisher King, and it goes something like this.

A prince goes out in search of adventure. Amorous adventure. Right away he gets in a fight with a dark knight, a pagan. During the clash the pagan gets killed and the prince gets a lance stuck through both balls. Ouch. Why did it have to be *both* balls?

Anyway, he becomes a king; but he's wounded in his "generative region," and because the health of the land and the king are connected, the land becomes a wasteland.

When I heard this story I thought, "For sure, that's where the Black Hole comes from. It's a wound inside people that's escaped into the trees." So I decided to let the Friends deal with the symbolic Black Hole while I got on the trail of the real one.

In the story of the Fisher King the wound gets worse and worse until the King can barely sit up in bed, and the only thing that eases his pain is fishing (hence the moniker). Then an innocent young fool called Parzival drops by to visit, and when he sees how much pain the King is in, he asks what the problem is. Immediately, this spontaneous act of compassion heals the wound, and the land flourishes.

The book I read suggested this interpretation: the original fight between the prince and the pagan is a clash between the spiritual and sensual parts of a person's soul. The sensual, animal part is killed off, and the spiritual part is mortally wounded. The healing occurs when the youthful, spontaneous part of the soul re-emerges into consciousness.

When I first read this story it sounded a chord. I figured it was pretty arcane stuff, but then I went to a new-age bookstore in Victoria and there was a whole Fisher King wall. Verily, 'twas an industry.

Now, one of my favourite parts in Parzival was where the knights went off on their quests, and each went into the forest where there was no path. In other words, it's a personal trip. So rather than add to the wall, I'm going to talk about the new ending of the Fisher King myth, which is what has been screwing me up.

A while back during a rainy spell I rented a couple of videos from the store, and watched them at Crabber Dave's. Both had Keanu Reeves in them.

The first movie was called *Little Buddha* (Keanu plays Buddha). Some Tibetan monks are testing kids to see which one of them is the reincarnation of their dead pal. Because it's the nineties one of the kids has to be a girl. Sure, why not. During the tests the life of the historic Buddha unfolds, except for the part where Buddha didn't want female disciples because he wasn't sure if women were cut out for Nirvana. That sort of detail puts the kibosh on the whole Buddha trip for me — I'm the kind of guy who likes to think that in heaven, anything goes.

Towards the end of the movie this crazy psycho guy called Kama tries to distract Buddha while he's trying to meditate. But Buddha says something like: "You can't distract me, bud. Because you *are* me." Aha! he's only a projection. Kama is welcomed back into Buddha's inner sanctum, and enlightenment ensues.

The second movie was called *Speed*. In this one a psychotic Dennis Hopper straps a bomb to a bus, and if it goes below 55 MPH — Kablooie! Commuter chips everywhere. Luckily, Keanu is on board, and he's a cop, trained to drive up the sides of buildings. But it's the nineties; in the name of gender equity, one of the women passengers (the prettiest one) has to drive, despite the fact that her license has been revoked. And even though she does a darn fine job, with Keanu coaching from the sidelines like some crazy Lamaze driving instructor, she still ends up chained to a pole, whence she is rescued by Keanu, as in days of yore. I guess this is the sort of thing that makes women tense. Well, no wonder. If I always ended up chained to a pole by a psycho, I'd be tense too. And as a matter of fact, I am tense. Sexually tense. Why? perhaps it's because from an early age I knew I wasn't Keanu. I was pretty sure I wasn't the woman chained to the pole. And that only left psychotic Dennis. Yep, tense is a polite word for what I am.

Now, I figure I could have saved a whack of cash by making two movies in one: Psychotic Dennis straps a bomb to Keanu's soul, and if he's not transcended by the end of the movie, KA-BLOOOIE! Kundalini sauce everywhere.

And while I was looking at *Speed* in this metaphysical light, I noticed that it's basically a souped-up Fisher King myth. See, as the story of *Speed* unfolds we discover that once upon a time psychotic Dennis was a cop, who was terribly injured in the line of duty. Keanu, the young fool, is supposed to heal his wounds with the magic question. But things go awry. Dennis is so psycho there's no way of reaching him. He has Black Holes for chakras, man. By the end of the flick they're wrestling on top of a train, like the prince and the pagan at the beginning of the Fisher King tale. And here's the ending, unforeseen by those twelfth century troubadors: instead of healing the old guy's wound with a spontaneous act of compassion, the young fool smashes his head off with a train signal box, which puts healing out of the question.

Maybe the story got jacknifed together to fit it into the 90-minute format. Maybe it's all part of a sinister plot to keep us from healing our psychic wounds. Who knows? But that summer I was dragged into a very strange adventure, and I ended up wrestling with myself on top of a train (not literally — but pretty close). The ending of my adventure was a complete shocker. My inner Keanu and my inner Dennis ended up on the same team. I can't tell you exactly what went down when I passed through that black hole; but I'll just say that there are times in life when you need Dennis on-side. After a thousand years of cutting him off, it felt a little strange to welcome even a tiny sliver of him back into the fold. But better inside me than projected onto some unconscious nutbar who might end up doing all sorts of damage.

Reabsorbing Dennis led me into a strange dreamscape. I dreamed I had committed some nameless crime, and an angry mob had chased me onto a dock. I thought, "I'm trapped!" But just then two women appeared, one with golden hair, another with dark hair. Both of them reminded me of my Anima. The dark haired woman began to sing. The golden haired woman twiddled the controls on a huge wall of recording equipment. Suddenly the dark woman's voice pierced the air with a note so pure it unearthed something at the bottom of the sea. Up from the water burst a strange, beautiful creature: a man with the head of a bear, his whole body ringed by a hairy golden halo. Strange though he was, I recognized him from somewhere. As he raced towards me over the tops of the waves I realized why. "My God," I thought. "It's Orange Ted!"

I was so surprised. Ted seized me and carried me to the shore some distance from the mob, and as we hit the beach our bodies fused and I ran up the sand like an animal, pumped to the max, ready to tango.

For the rest of the dream I was trying to reach my house. Although everyone was supposed to "get" me, every time I ran into someone they assisted me. It was like there was a giant conspiracy to help me get home. Finally the cops pulled me over. I figured it was the end of the line. But the main cop said into the radiophone that he'd got me in custody, and meanwhile he whispered, "I'll hold them off. Run."

"Jeez," I thought, "even the cops? This is nuts!"

When I awoke I had a strong feeling that I should run for mayor in the fall elections. I was as surprised as anyone. But it was the same sort of hunch that had told me to sleep off my seasickness during the sockeye trip, and that it would be okay to fall in love with River. It was an Inner Sanctum hunch, and I trusted it, even though running for mayor seemed like the craziest idea in the world.

So without really knowing what I was about, I drew up an election poster and stuck it up all over town. Then I waited to see what would happen.

CHAPTER NINE

Beer and Loafing on the Campaign Trail

ONCE, Tofino was a green tunnel with Chestermans Beach at one end and the Maquinna Pub at the other. Those days are gone. When our little town became the darling of the environmental industry, there was a tourism KAboom. Chestermans Beach was bought up by out-of-towners, clearcut, and stuffed with giant houses that looked like Pizza Huts. The pub was yuppified. The peelers' stage, brass pole, and terry-towel tablecloths were torn out. Now the place was awash in glass and oak, and the locals slouched uneasily under a pastel frieze of little clipper ships.

Saddest of all was the fate of the green tunnel. The land along the road into town was owned by a man named Hans, a wild German expatriate with a grey crew cut and no trigger finger. He was the kind of guy who always ends up taking out the psychic garbage. One day, he heard a rumour that town council was considering a bylaw that would ban all tree-cutting inside the village. So he got the jump on them by cutting down every tree on his property before they could legislate. He burned the trees in huge piles. He dug up the stubble with a giant back hoe. He didn't stop until he'd purged his property of every vestige of Mother Nature.

When I saw what he'd done I wanted to stand in the middle of the massacre and wave my arms and yell, "Look, Hans! No Mom!" It was so ironic. We'd saved Meares Island and clearcut the town. Now our village looked worse than the Black Hole. And not a protester in sight.

It was on the billboards and hydro poles of this little hamlet-cum-wasteland that my election posters suddenly appeared.

Since the Battle for Clayoquot Sound had heated up, the town had divided into two warring factions: the liberal, ecofriendly, "my shit doesn't stink" left and the conservative, beef-gobbling, log-till-you-drop right. There was no middle ground. With the elections coming up, the political situation was particularly tense. Imagine a runaway truck thundering down a mountain road while the driver's left and right hands battle over the steering wheel. As some dead Chinese guy said: "No good can come of this."

As you can imagine, my comic press-conference posters caused a bit of a fuss. The left hand was concerned that my buffoonery would screw up the election, just as my landlord Poole had done the last time. Poole had run for alderperson in a spirit of fun. Before the all-candidates' meeting, he ate a whack of mushrooms and babbled on about East Timor and "bicycle suburbs" until the crowd was in stitches. Then he withdrew from the race. But the ballots had already been printed, and 10 people voted for him anyway.

The left's serious candidate, Jane, lost by three votes. Everyone blamed Poole, which was not really fair. Anyone who voted Poole after that speech probably thought they were voting for a new swimming pool.

Quite a few serious lefties asked me to drop out before I pulled a Poole. My response was simple: "I am not Poole," I said.

The folks at city hall were equally alarmed. Town council was at that time run by the right hand of the community, the conservative faction, who were desperately trying to protect their tiny village from the giant green arm that had reached over the pass that summer and knocked them almost senseless.

The leader of the right is a man named Lefty. He was once mayor himself. Usually in a town of 1,000 people, the local bigwig would not be a national icon. But this is Tofino. Lefty was on the Second World War savings bonds. Perhaps you remember the stirring image: a little blond boy breaking away from his mom and running toward his dad, who is marching off to war with his hat and gun. That little kid is our Lefty.

These days, Lefty runs a chandlery on the dock. His store is the kind of store I loved best when I was a kid: beef jerky and pop at the front and a labyrinth at the back crammed with pulleys, ropes, and brass boat fittings. Lefty and I always waved when we saw each other in town. He seemed to like me. But the idea of me as mayor gave him the willies. I guess he pictured me playing hacky-sack in my chambers, getting stoned and losing the keys to the city. So he called the troops into action.

The incumbent was a man named Frank, a quiet, white-haired fellow who also ran the hospital. People accused him of being asleep at the wheel. Well, no wonder — he was trying to drive the hospital and the town at the same time. I'd be tired, too. Some day I figured an alderperson was going to wake up to find that their leg had been amputated because Frank had confused his two positions.

While Frank drowsed, the town was driven by his co-pilot, Ilsa, the municipal administrator. She had a vision for Tofino: clean water, parking aplenty, and porta-potties wherever more than three people were gathered together. A lot of folks were upset that she was running things because they hadn't elected her. (Actually, they hadn't elected Frank, either. He'd won by acclamation.) But I figured Ilsa was okay because she was very efficient, almost robotlike in her knowledge of the Municipal Act. Usually a robot makes an excellent team member — like Data on *Star Trek*. Only Ilsa was behaving more like HAL in *2001: A Space Odyssey*.

Ilsa loved bylaws. She'd even hired a man named Tex to enforce them. It was Tex's job to shovel sand on your beach fire as you played your guitar under the stars. He was also the man who would mastermind the demolition of the shacks on Poole's Land. And he had a bottle of vodka riding on Frank.

The conservative cabal met for strategy planning at Elsie's dry-cleaning store, next door to the organic food store. Elsie was an alderperson, and she was also Poole's neighbour. It was her complaint that had set the demolition bylaw in motion.

The right hand didn't know what to make of my campaign. Was I even serious?

I wasn't sure myself. I knew I didn't want to be mayor. What I wanted was to jump on the next plane for Scotland and find River. The prospect of wandering through the Highlands with the love of my life seemed so much more inviting than a three-year term of fluorescent-basted tedium. I mean, they only gave the protesters 60 days. But I figured the mayor should be someone who could figure out how to get the left and right hands to shake.

The battle between the left and right was complicated by the fact that the two teams had traded shadows, just as I was prone to do in relationships. The right saw the left as a bunch of welfare hippies. Actually, the left was well-heeled. The "welfare hippies" lay in the right's shadow. The conservative cabal's fathers had been gyppo loggers and fishermen, self-made types who would never have taken a handout. But nowadays a lot of right-minded folks are slaves for giant multinationals, and spend their winters blotto in front of the TV while the UIC cheques roll in with a steady no-no-no-yes-no.

This shadow is too painful to face, so they've traded it with the left. In return the left believes the right hand is wantonly destroying the planet with their greed, blind to the fact that they themselves are blasting from their jobs to their beach houses in shiny new cars. As long as the two teams are trading shadows, they need each other to remain as they are. Otherwise they'll have to fact the fact that they are their own worst enemies. While we fought among ourselves, giant out-of-town entities such as Greenpeace and Mac Blo were preparing to gobble us up and leave nothing but our ball caps. Healing town's split personality would not be easy. But I had a plan.

I had noticed a parallel between town's problems and the Fisher King story. The old redneck part of town had been badly gored and refused to deal with the wound. The young, hip part of town, instead of helping, was driving the knife deeper into the wound. If we weren't careful, our tale would have a Keanu conclusion. What we needed was a spontaneous act of compassion between the two parts of the town's psyche.

So I set out to become mayor, running my campaign like a perfect circle, refusing to cut out the bad bit — logging/protesting — and trying my best to behave spontaneously under the hot lights of politics. And I figured now that I'd completed my descent down through those mysterious chakras in my own life, from Head Office all the way out through the ominous Black Hole, I was poised to come full circle, back to the town's head office.

So, as the weeks passed, I told everyone that I wanted to represent all of town, no matter what their leanings were. Every day I walked into town and had coffee at the Common Loaf Bakery, bastion of the left. Then I'd go down and have a few beers at the pub. And soon word got around that my first objective was to bring town together.

It seemed almost hopeless — but lately I'd seen something new in the direction our culture was headed that encouraged me. See, every few weeks I got a long letter from River in Scotland. Her letters were covered in spirals. You know how it is with letters from a lover: I pored over them, took them to bed, and so on. The spirals invaded my dream world. They got into my belly. I saw spirals in water, in clouds — I even drew one on my kid's face.

That's when I began to feel that perhaps the West hadn't been moving in circles for the past 2,000 years after all. The circles were getting smaller, spiraling inwards to the centre. Circles are just circles, but

spirals are going somewhere. It took Christianity 1,000 years to get from the Crucifixion to the Inquisition. It took science only 300 to get from Newton's declaration that "God is reason" to Oppenheimer's A-bomb speech: "Now I am become Death, destroyer of worlds." Feminism made the rounds from "Women and men are equal" to "God is a woman, men are scumbags" in less than 30 years. And environmentalism has gone from the back burner to the limelight in less than 10. At this rate, the next great social movement will be compromised and mistrusted from day one. Hmmm . . . maybe it's the men's movement.

So we are approaching the eye in the centre of the western cyclone. I wasn't sure what would happen there, but suddenly things didn't seem so hopeless after all. And right around that time I learned something from my X-Wife that put it all in perspective. My X-Wife practised astrology. When we moved out here she dreamed of becoming an astrologer, consulting the book of the stars and explaining to the locals what would happen to them next. But to cover the bills, she ended up working for a whale-watching outfit. Now she sat behind a big desk that said ZODIACs, consulting a big schedule book and explaining to out-of-towners what would happen to them that afternoon. However, she still did astrology on the side.

One night, I was staying at her place and I read a book on astrology before I crashed. The book talked about the Great Year. Due to a slight wobble in Earth's rotation, the sun moves a little to the left against the background of stars each time it rises. Over about 24,000 years, it travels through every sign of the zodiac. The complete circle is called the Great Year.

Astrologers say our group consciousness is affected by the sign we're in. What caught my interest was that for the past 2,000 years, the sun has been rising in the sign of Pisces, symbolized by two fish swimming in opposite directions. Now, you don't have to be Joseph Campbell to figure that one out. The way I see it, one fish represents the good part of the circle of life: Christ, love, equality, wild salmon. The other fish represents the bad bit: the Antichrist, hate, oppression, farm salmon. Since the time of Christ, our psyches have been split and the pieces have been swimming in opposite directions. No wonder we've broken the circle of life. No wonder we've always divided into two teams and fought: America and Russia, left and right, Sonny and Cher —

But the Age of Pisces is almost over. That's why things are so extreme right now — everything's coming to a head. In a few years the sun will rise in Aquarius and a new age will dawn (that musical *Hair* was a little premature). The symbol for Aquarius is a person holding a jug of water — the Water Bearer. It's also a symbol for the self. Could it be that in this new age, the human psyche would be whole again, no longer torn in opposite directions, no longer driven to cut out the bad bit? I imagined a whole planet of Water Bearers, whole individuals with no need to find the disowned parts of their souls in an enemy. Things were looking up.

But I wasn't about to start explaining any of this to my logger pals.

So I put these strange visions into my Inner Sanctum for the time being and continued to play it by ear. My one and only election strategy was spontaneity. I walked into the Common Loaf each day and let it develop from there.

On the Monday before the election, we had our usual all-candidates' meeting. Everyone packed into the gym at the school. Frank read a little typed speech about what he'd do as mayor: house foreign dignitaries when they came to visit, represent the community, work to reduce polarization, and so on. When I got up, everyone was nervous that I would pull out my bag of jokes. This was the dragon I had to face: my compulsion to make a joke out of everything under the sun. I was nervous, too. I had prepared no speech. I had decided to wing it. I wasn't sure what I was going to say. I just planned on saying whatever occurred to me on the spur of the moment.

When they asked how I saw the position of mayor, I said I saw it as a cross between a chess game and being a dad. A chess game because now and then you had to sacrifice a piece to win the game — and as mayor I would sometimes have to make unpopular decisions. A dad because I figured you had to dote a bit on the town, put its needs first, and say every now and then, "I love you."

"And I do," I blurted out suddenly. "I love this town."

Thundering applause. I was startled. Everyone was startled. It looked like my days as town fool were over.

In this unexpected thaw I began to glance around the room and wonder if any one would actually vote for me. And you know - there was no right hand. There was no left hand. Just a bunch of folks I'd known for a long time.

By the end of the meeting, things looked pretty good for me. Lefty was perplexed. He was leaping around, swinging his arms as if he'd scarfed down a station wagon full of Count Chocula. Someone said to him, "Gee, it looks like Andrew might win."

"If he does," Lefty promised darkly, "I'll sell my house."

I thought, "This is like a high-stakes poker game. 'I'll see your house destroyed and I'll raise you mine.'"

When election day came I was calm, but dark fears were whizzing through my head like bikers at a county fair. City hall was like a war room. Tex screened everyone at the door. Ilsa buzzed around making sure there were no violations. Lefty sat at a big desk at the end of the room, like a pit bull with a ball cap, challenging every voter he didn't recognize. Around noon, Tim, who'd been born and raised just down the street from Lefty, showed up to vote for his first time. Lefty leaped up and cried "I challenge that vote! You don't live here!"

Someone whispered to him who it was. Lefty plunked himself down, disconsolate. "Damn kids grow up so fast you can't even recognize them," he grumbled sadly.

At five, the polls shut. Now the black box held the answer to the question on everyone's lips: Who was the mayor of Tofino?

Ilsa's husband, Blue, and Elsie's sister, Gilda, began to tally the votes. To their horror it was neck and neck. As the box emptied, with Frank ahead, then me, then Frank again, Blue began to panic. "I'll have to move!" he cried. "I can't live in a town that's run by a clown!"

In their zeal, the election officials discounted five votes for dubious reasons: two because they were in pen, two because there were no tails on the ticks, and one because the voter hadn't quite lifted

"You can kick a man out of the party... but you can't kick the party out of a man."

his pencil, and the bars of his X were joined by a faint line. Amazingly, all five were Andrew votes.

When the dust cleared, Frank had 326 votes. I had 320. Even with the five votes that had been discounted just for the heck of it, I was still a vote shy. Frank had won by a single vote — presumably his own. He was now self-appointed mayor of Tofino.

When I heard the results, I was flabbergasted. I'd set out to bring the town together and ended up cutting it exactly in half.

Everyone wanted me to ask for a recount. But after examining the evidence, I decided I'd lost fair and square. I figured it was time to bow out gracefully. I told my dismayed supporters not to worry. I said Frank could be the day mayor and I'd be their night mayor. I'd cover the night shift. Take out the psychic garbage. I'm good at that.

Press coverage of the election was pretty wild. The Port Alberni paper called me a militant environmentalist. *B.C. Report* called me the "little-known Green candidate who tried to hijack town council." The *Vancouver Sun* called me the winner. And the local hippie paper quoted me as saying I didn't mind losing because "I don't cling to things." Actually, what I'd said was: "I'm trying not to cling to things."

I was trying. I was trying not to cling to River. But I wasn't doing too well. The first thing I thought when I heard the results (after a brief pang of impotent rage) was that at last I'd be able to go find her. But two weeks later, when we talked on the phone, River said she wanted to let go of me.

I won't lie to you. I was bummed. I'd lost the election, I'd lost my dream house, and now I'd lost my love. Like sunrise on a train wreck, the awful truth dawned: I didn't care about humiliation at the polls, or about my house getting torn down. I didn't care about anything except getting River back. The clamor of the mayorship battle had served to drown out the small voice which was whispering from my Inner Sanctum, "Time to let go." Spring was over, long gone. And River was gone too.

Winter came on strong that year. The Black Hole welled up inside me till my soul felt like a green fringe around a charnel pit. Unable to break with tradition, in the butt-end of the year I ran out of cash and had to go down to the fish plant, where not much had changed, except that the three ladies from Port had been replaced by a giant bloodsucking machine. I wept my way through each shift, with my ball cap pulled down to hide my eyes and the fish-gut grinder masking my sobs. But I knew the Black Hole was a part of me. I figured spring would come again and something new would grow in the heart of all that darkness, if I could only let go and pass through the pain.

So I let go of River, and she swam out of my life as naturally as she had entered it. But she left one thing behind: a vision of two people paddling a green canoe somewhere out in the sound. The guy in front looks a bit like me, except he has horns. The woman in back is young and beautiful, and her hair streams out behind her, golden. A young child peeks over the side of the canoe at the clear blue water. These folks live in a little cabin on a long, sandy beach, way out in the sound. They have always lived there. And they always will.

At last, spring came. The geese flew overhead. River wrote to say she was falling in love with someone and they were moving to a farm in Ireland. She sounded really happy.

A few nights later, I was drowsing by my wood stove and I had one of those waking dreams — not quite asleep, no longer awake. In this dream I saw the beginning of the Age of Aquarius. I saw the Water Bearer with a huge jug of water that held the world's soul. I gazed at the clay sides of the jug, and for a moment it was as if I could see through them. Inside it was full of clear blue water, and in the water there were two silver fishes — and they were swimming in opposite directions.

MONTHS passed. River still flowed through my dreams and daydreams. The trip to the Megin glowed like Eden two summers behind me, and I was in exile. I had glimpsed something sacred in her face, and fishy zodiacal epiphanies aside, I had no idea how to embrace that mystery.

To distract myself from the pain I wrote a long story about the things I'd seen in Clayoquot Sound and published it in a Vancouver magazine. The environmental movement saw their shadow walking around under the hot lights of media coverage, freaked, and fired a salvo in my direction. I was unconcerned. Compared with losing River, the slings and arrows of outraged eco-warriors didn't hurt at all.

I spiralled into the deepest sorrow of my life. By the fall it was all I could do to sit up in bed.

Of course, that's when city hall closed in for the kill. They sent Poole a notarized letter saying I had three weeks to bring my house up to code. (Poole was just heading south to California for a month, so he put it on a backburner. Luckily, I read all about it in the paper.)

Now, it's been my experience that when you build a dream house/bush pyramid for your Anima using living trees as a foundation, you can pretty well forget about the whole code thing. A quick visit to city hall confirmed my fears: it would be more practical to bring my kid's dollhouse up to code and live in *it*. In desperation I tried to hire some helicopter loggers to lift my house to safety, but they didn't want to be liable. I thought vaguely about a standoff, but in my case it could only last three days, because then I'd have to go pick up my kid from her mom's.

So I found an apartment on the top floor of a condemned house right by the fish plant, with floors that sloped like the villain's hideout in *Batman*, a Stockhausen water heater, and a young deckhand downstairs called Dave who cranked world beat music until the wee hours every night. Then I carried all my possessions back down that long, muddy trail. It was kind of disheartening. If the gods really wanted to sock it to Sisyphus they'd make him carry the rock downhill for all eternity and have it roll back up.

Just to cap it all off, that same week my big pal Leo pulled up stakes and left town for good. I couldn't believe it. He was some of the last human old-growth around. I just sort of figured he would always live in his house on the inlet, with his moose racks and guns. He had such great finishing power. I thought he'd be the last to go. But gone he was, leaving only the sinister-looking hole he'd smashed in the drywall with his head that night 10 years ago, when this adventure began.

As soon as I got set up I lay down on my new couch and slept for a couple of months. I was massively bummed. The winter weeks passed in a dream. I listened to CBC Radio, slept, stared out the window, slept, dozed, day-dreamed, crashed, slept again. It was like diving into a bottomless well. This must be what it's like to drink yourself to death, I thought.

But it wasn't long before I noticed how nice the little old house by the fish plant felt. It wasn't much to look at, but it was warm and snug, like a cocoon, and the old wooden floors were like a library of good memories. Then one night I was lying in the dark listening to the giant old hi-fi that was there when I moved in, watching the glow of the electric coil heater, and bemoaning my fate as an off-the-grid refugee, when I realized that I felt quite at home. In fact, I felt like the real dream house was inside my body, and the pyramid on the hill was only a copy.

Outside, storms raged. I concentrated on making lunches for my kid, dropping her off at school, picking her up, and splashing in all the puddles on the way home. That's all I did. It was like submerging myself in the Ocean of Women, which didn't look so bad right then — it looked like a safe refuge from the terrible storm that was tearing Head Office apart.

Deep, deep underwater I got a glimpse of why I have such trouble welcoming back sacred parts of my soul: maybe the finishing power I'd been looking for was female. What I needed to complete the hero's journey was a goddess in my inner sanctum. She's the welcoming committee. Without her those projections just wander around the planet causing all sorts of mischief. And it does seem like there's been a lot of mischief lately.

But who can say? It's certainly mysterious. When I think about the environmental movement, what I recall most clearly is that strange tree of fish back at Sulphur Pass. And although I accused Jesus of cutting out the animal part of the human soul, I remember now that he was born right in among the animals. Maybe it's all some big conspiracy involving the whole planet. What if all this time Africa has remembered the perfect circle of life, Asia has divided the circle, and the West has broken the circle so that it could be changed into a spiral?

Nahh. Too far-fetched. Anyway, I built a big shrine in my front room to the Goddess, and spent a little time with her every morning. Around solstice I bobbed up to the surface and saw that things weren't so bad. I still had my kid, and my body was in one piece.

Just as I began to cheer up, my new landlord, a huge Brit with a rugby attitude towards life, dropped by to tell me he was worried about me living in a condemned building. The front stairs were falling apart — in fact, the only reason they were still standing was because they were propped up by an abandoned refrigerator underneath. Someone was going to get hurt on those stairs, and he didn't want to be liable. What he wanted was to turn the whole house over to the local volunteer fire department so they could use it to practise on. We had a nice chat, and I agreed to leave in two weeks.

On the second day of spring the local fire department, including young Dave from downstairs, torched the old house by the fish plant. First they filled it with smoke and crawled around inside, rescuing dummies from cupboards and so on. Then they started a practice fire, but it got out of hand and the whole place went up in flames. I went down to visit the next day, and the only thing left standing was the front stairs, still suppported by the old fridge, sticking up into space.

It was a beautiful day: clear blue sky, with a gentle westerly breeze. One of those great spring days when you feel it would be no problem if your life caught fire and you escaped wearing only your underpants. So I kicked around the ruins and wondered what lay around lovely Gaia's next curve.

For my immediate family:
Hazel, Graham, Moira and David
It was nuclear — but at least it wasn't Chernobyl.

Thanks to these fellow adventurers:

Parvizals: Dave Hurwitz, Neil McQueen, Doug Berry, Jan Janzen,
Bill Morrison, Dan Flynn, Ralph Tieleman, Aaron Marshall, Jeff
Beylard, Philippe Correia, Freddy Gutmann, Stewart, Donovan
Grail Maidens: Kirstin McLaren, Jasmine Mitchell, Patty O'Stone,
Joanna Gislason, Leslie Bader, Crystal Heald, Shell Windsor
Fisher Kings: Barry Grumbach, Michael Poole, Brian Kimola
Gueneveres: Gwen Davies, Therese Bouchard, Jen Susheil
Lao Tzu types: Laser Dave, Frank Harper, Al Anderson,
Ann Manning, Kal Kan
Head Office crew: Charles Campbell, Sid Tafler, Kathy Shaw, Gary
Shaw, Adrienne Mason, Kara Shaw, Terry Glavin, Rolf Maurer

Transmontanus is edited by Terry Glavin
Designed and produced by Val Speidel
Printed and bound in Canada by Best Book Manufacturers
1   2   3   4   5   99   98   97   96   95

Please direct submissions and editorial enquiries to: Transmontanus, Box C-25, Fernhill Road, Mayne Island, B.C. V0N 2J0. All other correspondence, including sales and distribution enquiries, should be sent to New Star Books, 2504 York Avenue, Vancouver, B.C. V6K 1E3.

Publication of this book is made possible by grants from the Canada Council and the Cultural Services Branch, Province of British Columbia.

CATALOGUING IN PUBLICATION DATA

Struthers, Andrew.
  The green shadow

  (Transmontanus, ISSN 1200-3336; v. 3)
  ISBN 0-921586-44-2

  1. Struthers, Andrew, 1961– 2. Tofino (B.C.) — Biography. 3. Green movement — BritishColumbia — Humor 4. Clayoquot Sound Region (B.C.) — Environmental conditions.
I. Title. II. Series.
FC3849.T63S77 1995   971.1   C95-910615-4
F1089.5.T63S77 1995